A PRACTICAL GUIDE

—— to ——

FACILITATING SUBSTANCE USE DISORDER RECOVERY

Geri Miller

cognella®

SAN DIEGO

Bassim Hamadeh, CEO and Publisher
Amy Smith, Associate Editorial Manager
Abbey Hastings, Senior Production Editor
Emely Villavicencio, Senior Graphic Designer
Kylie Bartolome, Licensing Specialist
Natalie Piccotti, Director of Marketing
Kassie Graves, Senior Vice President, Editorial
Alia Bales, Director of Editorial and Production

Cover and interior image: Copyright © 2022 iStockphoto LP/stellalevi.

Printed in the United States of America.

The excerpts from Twelve Steps and Twelve Traditions are reprinted with permission of Alcoholics Anonymous World Services, Inc. ("A.A.W.S."). Permission to reprint these excerpts does not mean that A.A.W.S. has reviewed or approved the contents of this publication, or that A.A.W.S. necessarily agrees with the views expressed herein. A.A. is a program of recovery from alcoholism only – use of these excerpts in connection with programs and activities which are patterned after A.A., but which address other problems, or in any other non-A.A. context, does not imply otherwise.

cognella | ACADEMIC PUBLISHING
320 South Cedros Ave., Ste. 400, Solana Beach, CA 92075

This book is dedicated to Ron Hood, my husband and best friend, who was there through it all, and

my families—

Gale, Abby, and Jason Miller; Tom, Laura, Natalie, and Kate Prow; Zoe, Anrai, and Corina Schriver;

Pat Mitchell Anderson's children: Mary, Shelley, Marnie, Scott, and Tim; Marilou, Richard, Alan, Lorie, Ted, and Dan Steinmetz; and the women, my "sisters" who were with me from the beginning: Judy Erickson, Pat Mitchell Anderson, and Judy Retterath.

It is also dedicated to the many SUD professionals, my students (graduate and undergraduate), who I have trained over the years. You have taught me so much about the SUD field and helped encourage my passion and commitment to this important life-saving work through your passion and commitment to it. Such wonderful experiences we have shared.

Finally, this book is dedicated to all the SUD clients and their loved ones who I had the honor of counseling; all those who have lived with or are living with the disease of SUD as well as those who have died from the disease; and the helping professionals who remain committed to this important, sometimes miraculous, life-saving work, who, like me, have witnessed the miracles of recovery in the person with SUD and their loved ones.

Listen to the wind, *it talks*.
Listen to the silence, *it speaks*.
Listen to your heart, *it knows*.

—Native American Proverb

Brief Contents

Contents

ACTIVE LEARNING

This book has interactive activities available to complement your reading.

Your instructor may have customized the selection of activities available for your unique course. Please check with your professor to verify whether your class will access this content through the Cognella Active Learning portal (http://active.cognella.com) or through your home learning management system.

If you are not reading this book as part of a course, the Active Learning companion can be purchased separately for independent study at https://store.cognella.com/70768-1a-001

cognella® | ACTIVE LEARNING content

Preface

I have written this book with the intention of providing a book on substance use disorder (SUD) recovery that is practical and unique in its perspective. The book is meant to be a "how to" manual that assists the reader in the diagnosis, assessment, and treatment of SUD. It is an attempt to reduce the confusion that exists with SUD by providing a pragmatic, balanced perspective. It is a comprehensive, condensed book of practical approaches for the SUD helping professional.

In recent years, many individuals have entered the SUD field from a variety of helping professional fields (e.g., mental health, medical, legal) and paraprofessional fields (e.g., peer recovery specialists). The purpose of the book is to introduce readers to the philosophy, approaches, and "culture" of effective SUD professional work. It provides practical information that is anchored in both clinical observations and in research. Because many experienced SUD professionals have left the field (e.g., quitting, retiring) who would have mentored in a new generation of SUD professionals, this book contains both a historical perspective and current information about the SUD field.

The hope is this book will assist professionals from various fields in expanding their perspective of SUD work through the provision of a combination of "tried and true" information about SUD counseling with novel information and approaches. Hence, there are sections in this book that the reader may disagree with. The contents of this book may stir controversy by simply providing information that is novel to the reader or does not fit the application to their clinical population.

As a result, the book chapters are designed to both provide information and facilitate application of the information. All chapters contain the following components: open with a Stress Management Tip, share the story of a person in SUD recovery, and close with Interactive Reader Components (e.g., case studies, exercises, appendices, suggested readings/resources). Throughout the text, boxes, figures, tables, and appendices are used to highlight important points.

With regard to specific chapter information:

- **Chapter 1** provides information that can be integrated with the reader's knowledge base. Specifically, in this chapter, there is discussion of the author's preparation in writing the book, orientation to the chapter in terms of a suggested reading approach, and a summarization of the culture of SUD counseling in terms of its evolution and philosophy. There is a specific emphasis on describing the active SUD brain, the contributing factors to substance use from the perspective of the biopsychosocial model, and various intervention components that facilitate the development of the recovering SUD brain.

- **Chapter 2** opens with a discussion in the chapter overview of the potential for a helping professional to develop a "stigmatic lens" through which the person with SUD is viewed. The discussion is followed by a presentation of the SUD recovery colloquial expressions (i.e., *addictionary*) of Alcoholics Anonymous (AA). The chapter also focuses on assisting the reader in the integration of the knowledge/experience of paraprofessionals and professionals, emotional sobriety concepts helpful to the person with SUD, and formation on how recovery communities of group counseling and self-help groups (e.g., AA) can assist the person in recovery in the development of a balanced lifestyle that consists of serenity and hope. There is also a special section on the impact of technology on AA.

- **Chapter 3** explores the overlapping concepts of self-care, creativity, and creative techniques as well as guidelines for the use of such creative techniques. The specific techniques are anchored in a review of the literature and a description of the techniques as they relate to each of the following four areas: story/metaphor; humor; experiential activity/play; and music.

- **Chapter 4** provides a further exploration of the four-legged stool of self-care presented in Chapter 3. Examination of the fourth leg of the stool (e.g., mind, emotions, spirit) stresses the importance of the person in SUD recovery developing a spiritual dimension to their recovery in order to have a balanced recovery lifestyle (i.e., broaden their life perspective and deepen the meaning of their lives).

The Conclusion section is a summary of the author's hopes for the reader and a closing to the text.

Acknowledgments

I have had excellent professional role models in the SUD counseling field—so many that I cannot name all of them who helped me develop a "head" and a "heart." To all of you who helped me develop both personally and professionally: You know who you are. You spent time explaining basic concepts of working in this field to me, you challenged me to be the best therapist, researcher, teacher, and person I could be, and you never settled for less in me or gave up on me. Thank you from the core of my being.

I am also deeply grateful to the SUD helping professionals and the students I have trained. To you, I say: You were brave with me by stepping away from the ease of technology and, instead, engaging in messy, genuine, human dialogue with me that allowed us, through community, to learn and grow together as we explored the field of SUD. You give and have given meaning to my life by allowing me the honor of teaching you.

I also want to thank the people at Cognella who believed I could write this book and supported me as I did so over a number of years. Kassie Graves, my editor, and Amy Smith, my project editor, believed in the importance of this work and were patient with me by repeatedly extending deadlines and never giving up on me. Kassie, an exceptional editor, waited for years for a product from me, always believing I would write this book and believing in its importance. Kassie also supported, encouraged, and trusted my creativity and my writing skills as well as providing excellent suggestions that improved this work. Amy met with me monthly for over a year and kindly supported me via Zoom with her words, caring presence, and delightful sense of humor. I looked forward to every meeting with her. To Tiffany Mok and her advertising team, and Emely Villavicencio, Senior Graphic Designer, a heartfelt thank you for making this book appealing in its appearance because as human beings: "We hear what we see." Emely revised her beautifully designed cover at least 7 times in response to my requests-she responded to these requests quickly and with amazing patience. To Haley Brown and Dr. Rachel Mann, who assisted me in the development of the Active Learning Site materials: "I thank you for your brilliant suggestions and willingness to collaborate respectfully with me on the all the teaching components that assist students in learning the material from as many avenues as possible (e.g., videos) and their professors in using the book to augment their professional knowledge base and assist them in their classroom teaching (e.g., PowerPoint; test questions, assignments)." The three of us had great fun in our creative collaborations on Zoom. Holly Russell, my copy editor, made precise, respectful comments that improved this book immensely. Abbey Hastings, my production editor, who in her thorough, organizing manner helped me meet the deadline that allowed this book to be published "on time". Every one of these individuals were a gift to me in the journey of writing this book.

To George Dennis, my computer teacher who helped me reliably for hours every week with computer struggles, word crafting, figures/boxes/tables/appendices, and most of all provided me with reliable support, I say: "Thank you for being one of the kindest, smartest, most patient people I have ever known. Without your endless support and your belief in me, this book would never have happened. George, your incredible sense of humor made our work enjoyable and a highlight in my life." Also, George's partner, Kate Hoffman, their dog Henry (the awesome parti poodle), and their adventuresome kitten Harley Quinn deserve a special "Thank you" for bringing joy and laughter to my life as I wrote this book. To Allie Reagan and Ali Kent, members of the "research team" with George and myself, I want to say to you: "Thank you for your kind hearts and brilliant minds that provided me with research and emotional support. You were committed, reliable 'employees'." And yes, the four of us (Allie, Ali, George, and I) are the "best research team in the world." We believed in the importance of our work and cared for each other. To Julie Gall, the graphic designer (e.g., cartoonist) who is one of the brightest and most delightful artists I have ever met: "Thank you for showing up in my life unexpectedly and sharing your many gifts with me. It was a gift and an honor to work with you." Reese Wells, with his kindness, patience, and brilliance created a podcast on this book.

A special "Thank you" also to:

- Barry Timberlake, who served as a consultant to me on many aspects of this book: Barry, this book could not have been written without you and your wonderful head and heart that are filled with knowledge, compassion, and hope for those who struggle with SUD.

- Russell Melillo, who was an invaluable consult to me on the "addictionary" components of this text: Russ, thank you for being patient with me as you educated me based on your knowledge and expertise.
- John Duggan, my friend, my colleague, who served as a teacher resource consultant in the development of Active Learning materials associated with this book: John, you are simply one of the brightest, kindest, compassionate, and supportive people I have ever known. You are a gift in my life.
- Jodi Cash, my trainer, who listened, gave me feedback, and asked questions about this book for the entire time I wrote: I deeply appreciate your reliability, loyalty, and honesty.
- Dawn Houck, one of my heroines in life, and her son, Gerald Houck, two people of the highest integrity and decency that I have ever met: You have sustained me through hard times and helped me enjoy life with your wonderful sense of humor.
- My wonderful Appalachian Mountain friends who share my values of family, community, and tradition with a spirit of honesty and humor.

To my friends, who I consider family, Bruce Kaplan and JoJo Muldoon (and their dog Otis, who passed away during the writing of this book, a human being who happened to be in a dog's body); Laurie Percival Oates; and Marilou, Richard, Alan, and Lorie Steinmetz: You hold a special place in my heart because each of you has shown me (and many others) kindness and compassion and created a safe place for me (and others) that encourages us to "show up for life" and never give up no matter what happens. I will always be in your debt.

I also appreciate the support from my Saturday morning coffee-drinking buddies, who stay with me on this adventure called life by helping me "live life on life's terms" (e.g., listening to me; being honest with me in a loving, supportive way; giving me hugs when I need them) and insisting I enjoy the gift of life with them through laughter and humor.

To my buddies and mentors who have left this world, Judy Erickson, Pat Mitchell Anderson, and Judy Retterath, pioneers in the SUD field who cared for and helped innumerable patients with SUD and their families, I say: Thank you. I love you, and I will miss all of you until I too leave this world.

To three incredible women who I think of as family, Laura Prow, Zoe Schriver, and Marnie Maroney, I say: You are incredible women both personally and professionally and are natural healers in the world who helps others (me included) feel safe and loved and comforted. I extend a special heartfelt "Thank you" to you.

Finally, to my husband and best friend, Ron Hood, who again demonstrated his love and support by reading every word written in every draft and who never stopped believing in me or asking for the highest work quality from me, I say, as I have said before: Thank you, Ron, for being on this life path with me. I love you. You are the best buddy ever. Also, a special thank you to Maggie, our Appalachian Mountain coon dog who made us laugh every day, and Hope, our 5-year-old black cat with the longest legs I have ever seen. Hope, who loves the outdoors as much as me, listened to me read the book out loud as I wrote it on the porches of our farm house from April 15, 2023, until the present time and who seemed to enjoy being on camera, as evidenced in the videos where he would show up uninvited, requiring them to be reshot. One of these videos, the "mishap video" posted on the Active Learning Site, is an example of a video that needed to be reshot. Both Maggie and Hope were the inspiration for the characters in the comic graphic design on the Active Learning Site.

Maggie was a "force of nature" who entered our lives and stayed with us for over 13 years. She had BIG eyes, a BIG nose, a BIG jaw, freckles, and legs that could bend in all directions as well as smelling like gingerbread. She was put to sleep due to cancer that erupted in her body shortly before this book went into production. "Maggie, we will miss you every day of our lives because you were a human being who happened to be a dog. You showed us the importance of love and loyalty and reliability." To Carrie Baarns, who is the manager of the Revisions and Author Care division of Cognella: "Thank you for your kind card expressing the sorrow of everyone at Cognella for our loss of Maggie. We will keep your handwritten personal note forever."

INTRODUCTION

OBJECTIVES

1. To understand the active substance use disorder brain.
2. To understand what leads to substance use.
3. To understand intervention components.

Overview of the Chapter

Examination of addiction (e.g., substance use disorder) in the United States results in confusion that stems from conflicting information regarding public policy, public interest, overdose deaths, and substance use. The difficulty in developing public policy in terms of the use of substances reflects the tendency of Americans to view addiction with both fascination and horror (Ross & Collins, 2010). This struggle with drug policy development occurs simultaneously with the decrease in the broad public interest in addiction and a sharp rise in drug overdose deaths (Odabaş, 2022). These drug overdose deaths—92,000 in 2020 (30% more than in 2019 and 75% more in the last 5 years)—are the highest annual total on record according to the Centers for Disease

Control and Prevention (Gramlich, 2022). Black male overdose deaths have increased substantially to the same level of overdose deaths as American Indian or Alaska Native men (Gramlich, 2022). Also, this confusion is compounded by the fact that (a) 2020 survey results in which 58.7% of individuals 12 or older reported that in the last month they had used tobacco, alcohol, or an illicit drug (Substance Abuse and Mental Health Services Administration [SAMHSA], 2021) and (b) marijuana and hallucinogen use in young adults is at the highest level in 2021 since 1988 (National Institute on Drug Abuse [NIDA], 2022). SAMHSA (2022) findings for this same age grouping showed 59.8% reported use of tobacco, vaped nicotine, used alcohol or used an illicit drug. SAMHSA (2022) findings also grouped individuals with SUD from *highest to lowest* as follows: *young adults* (aged 18-25; 27.8% or 9.7 million people) *adults aged 26 or older* (16.6% or 36.8 million people) and *adolescents aged 12-17* (8.7% or 2.2 million people). Throughout the world, in many countries, youth are using more substances than the previous generation, and in the 15–64 age range there has been a 20% increase in usage in 2020 (United Nations Office on Drugs and Crime, 2022).

This chapter will hopefully reduce the amount of confusion that can be a natural outcome of the examination of substance use disorder. Three areas will initially be presented in order to facilitate the integration of the information to the reader's knowledge base: author preparation for writing this book; chapter orientation [placed in the section "Suggested Approach for Reading this Chapter"]; and substance use disorder professional culture [labeled "Culture of Substance Use Disorder Work"].

Author Preparation for Writing This Book

I spent the last 5 years preparing for this book by telling people I encountered in everyday living (e.g., locally, nationally) that I was writing a book on addiction. I asked them (e.g., lay people, professional people) to tell me what *they* wanted to know about addiction and addiction recovery, not necessarily what the experts believed they should know. (Although experts were consulted in a survey sent out via the publisher, and their opinions also shaped this book.) I asked lay and professional individuals for their views because I wanted to anchor this book in the "voices of people" as well as recommendations of experts and research findings. I used the term "addiction" because in these everyday encounters, everyone (including the professionals) tended to default to this term rather than "substance use disorder" even when I began with the latter term. I was (and continue to be) impressed with the seriousness with which they considered my request (e.g., the time and energy they took to respond) and the personal sharing they did with a total stranger that often resulted in their sharing a powerful story about someone they knew (e.g., loved) who struggled with and/or died from addiction. Some of their stories, woven throughout this book, are combined with stories I have heard as a mental health provider. This approach respects individuals' confidentiality and protects them and their family members from the discrimination that accompanies this "disease of addiction" (Canning, 2021). Table 1.1 displays the thoughtful questions they asked, the wisdom they shared with me about what they had learned, and my responses of hopeful information to their concerns and interest in addiction.

I end this section with three suggestions for you, the reader, to consider:

- Establish a real, genuine, caring, honest relationship with people with SUD that is based on listening, not judging.
- Assist them in setting up communities of support similar to the one they have with you.
- Trust that this book will assist you in knowing enough to do this type of work by providing you with information and interventions on SUD that is both research-based and practically applicable.

I hope this information is useful to the reader. Also, because this work with patients with SUD can be stressful, a stress management tip is noted here. Practical, useful stress management tips will be provided in each chapter.

TABLE 1.1 Summary of "Voices of the People"

	Questions asked regarding specific topics	Wisdom learned regarding specific topics	Responses of hopeful information regarding specific topics
How they (people with SUD) "see the world" and "give meaning to the world"	- Why do they use substances? - Why don't they see themselves as addicted? - How can a substance be so consuming that they give up their lives for it? - Why is it so hard for them to stop?	- You can tell them about addiction, but something inside them has to be open to seeing things differently. - They need to want help. - Substance use is a coping mechanism.	- Because in active addiction their focus on the substance narrows their worldview and gives meaning to their world; in recovery they need to broaden their worldview and meaning. - The "hallmark of addiction" is that they continue to use in spite of negative consequences.
Compassionate accountability (compassion for their story balanced with accountability for their behaviors)	- What is the "wake-up call"? - What is the "trigger(s)" to waking up? - When does a person have enough?	- You need to understand it to get rid of it. - Hold them accountable for their behavior.	- They need to receive a welcoming message that invites hope they can recover from the SUD. - We need to remember that "kindness may be a stranger to them" and they deserve ordinary human kindness no matter what choices they have made or the circumstances in which they find themselves. - They need to be held accountable for their behaviors while also receiving compassion for their story that led to the SUD.
The "can't" and "won't" of change	- How long do you wait for them to change/get sober? - How many chances do you give them to sober up before you give up?	- They are powerless. - No one says as a child, "I want to grow up and have a substance use disorder." - No one is proud to have a SUD.	- Can't: They are caught in the throes of the SUD (e.g., the powerlessness where they "can't change"). - Won't: They are protecting their supply (e.g., see the substance as the solution for all their problems).

Education wanted in these areas	Biopsychosocial model:	Biopsychosocial model:	Biopsychosocial model:
	-Is it automatically passed on in a family? Will I get the disease too? -Are sensitive people more vulnerable to SUD? Do they need to learn to work on their sensitivity instead of turning to alcohol/drugs? -Is grief a trigger for using alcohol/drugs? Assessment: -What are the markers of addiction? -When does someone "cross over the line"? Treatment: -How do they get over it? -How do people come off of heroin and those other drugs (opiates)? -How do you tell them about treatment options? -Are support groups like Alcoholics Anonymous a crutch?	-It is hard to understand addiction if you are not addicted. -Addiction can happen fast. -Addiction changes a person. -People with SUD always lie. -Opiates are bad. -It is hard on families and others who care about people with SUD. Assessment: -It is a sensitive subject. People don't want to talk about it because they are worried about what others will think and say. Treatment: -It is like any chronic, life-threatening disease. -Rehab should be cheaper and easier to access.	-Discuss the biopsychosocial model to assist in understanding the onset and maintenance of the SUD as well as the recovery from the SUD. -Inform them of sources such as NIDA, NIAAA, and SAMHSA that provide reliable information that is current, practical, and research-based. Assessment: -They needed an experienced, credentialed assessor to determine if they have an SUD. -Inform them of sources such as NIDA, NIAAA, and SAMHSA that provide reliable information that is current, practical, and research-based. Treatment: -When confused about an intervention, switch it to another life-threatening, chronic illness (e.g., cancer, heart disease) and ask how relapse might happen. -Inform them of sources such as NIDA, NIAAA, and SAMHSA that provide reliable information that is current, practical, and research-based. -Detach with love. Don't attack them or cut them out of your life.

BOX 1A: STRESS MANAGEMENT TIP

HALT Self-Care "Inspection" Checklist

	Problem		"Repair" estimate [time/energy/money Cost]
Am I **H**ungry?	Yes	No	_____
Am I **A**ngry?	Yes	No	_____
Am I **L**onely?	Yes	No	_____
Am I **T**ired?	Yes	No	_____

Additionally, each chapter will conclude with a quote that may be a possible source of hope to the reader who is working in a field that can be discouraging in many ways. For example, professionals may experience their own sense of powerlessness over the "disease"; their clients/patients with SUD and their loved ones; and the professional's work environment barriers to serving the best interests of their clients/patients.

Recovery Story

"I was alone and did not know where to turn for help."

The Story Behind the Statement

A pretty, smart woman with a face that looked like nothing terrible had happened to her said to a helping professional, "I think I have a problem with pot because I smoke it every day and I cannot stop using it." The professional asked her about her use of substances and her life (e.g., work, family, friends). By having a caring, real, genuine, and honest dialogue with her and listening carefully (avoiding assumptions and the appearance she had it "all together"), the professional was able to draw out the real picture of her: a lonely, frightened young woman using substances to help her cope with her life struggles (no family support, no sober friends, and only a job with a few people who cared about her). She had few inner and outer resources and was unsure she wanted to quit using substances. She felt welcomed and hopeful as a result of their short but meaningful conversation where the professional showed kindness and respect and made a commitment to help her explore her problems. As a result, she shared specific details of her history: She started using substances in college with her friends because she did not know how to live in this "college world" that was so far from the poverty, violence, and alcoholism in which she was raised. Moving away from her college friends to a major city in order to have a job, she found herself alone with no one to turn to help her cope with all the changes and her unresolved trauma from her childhood. She made new friends who also used substances heavily in order to cope with living with her new life's demands and increasingly found herself caught in a powerlessness over her use of substances. This professional provided her with a "stronghold"—a place of security that had strong defenses from the outside world, a place where she felt safe. Because of her experience with the helping professional, she embarked on an initially frightening journey of self-exploration that led to an increasing number of strongholds: caring relationships with others and a community of support for staying sober as she continued to live life on life's terms. She never relapsed back to substance use during 4 decades of being sober.

Author Personal Reflections

This "true story" (a compilation of stories from different individuals with whom I have worked) highlights that there are simply times when the world asks too much of us and we are especially vulnerable to our own "soft spots" and the influences of forces outside of ourselves. The opening statement captures a powerlessness, a hopelessness where we turn to comforts outside of ourselves, and these comforts may be harmful (substances) or healing (helping professionals). This story shows what can happen to a human being who turns to substances to help them live with life's terms, and it also shows that there is hope for people with substance use disorder and that we, as helping professionals, can make a significant difference in a person's life story in even our shortest encounters.

Suggested Approach for Reading This Chapter

The information in this chapter is provided in the theoretical context of transactional analysis (TA; Berne, 1964). *Transactional analysis* refers to "analyzing the transactions within the individual and between individuals" (Miller, 2024, p. 73). A visual illustration of this theory is in Figure 1.1.

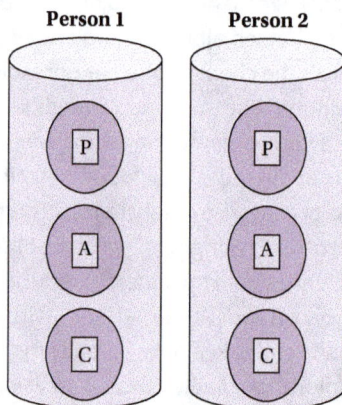

Websites
1) The International Transactional Analysis Association
   https://www.itaaworld.org/about-itaa
2) The United States of America Transactional Analysis Association
   https://www.usataa.org/

FIGURE 1.1   Transactional Analysis

In the context of this chapter, the interaction examined is that between the author and the reader, as italicized below in Miller's (2024) explanation of Figure 1.1:

> Each cylinder represents an individual. Within each person is a parent (P), adult (A), and child (C). The internal parent guides/directs us. The internal adult is the rational, negotiating aspect of ourselves that mediates between the internal parent and the internal child. The internal child is the most vulnerable, needy, childlike aspect of ourselves. Each internal aspect (P, A, C) interacts

with the other internal aspects of ourselves (P, A, or C) and these interactions can be positive or negative. ...

Each person has their own internal dialogue occurring, and these internal dialogues impact the transactions between individuals. (pp. 73–74)

The author is encouraging the reader to approach the chapter information, in TA terms, from an adult state ("I have my own views about substance abuse disorder recovery") as the author presents the information from an adult state ("These are my views about substance use disorder recovery"). That means that the author is respecting the reader's right to decide whether the information presented fits the population and the setting of their clients with SUD. Thus, the self-help group adage of "Take what you like and leave the rest" is encouraged while reading this information. Take in and adapt the information presented to your professional style, setting, and client population.

Culture of Substance Use Disorder Work

Increasingly individuals have entered the SUD field from a variety of helping professional fields (e.g., mental health, medical, legal) and paraprofessional fields (e.g., peer recovery specialists) and practice their professional orientation work in the SUD field. This coincides with numerous experienced SUD professionals leaving the field (e.g., quitting, retiring). In combination, these two tendencies have resulted in a cultural shift in the SUD field. *Culture*, here, is defined as our view of the world that is shaped by our personal and professional experiences that impact how we assess SUD and the action we take in response to it (Miller, 2021). In order to understand this cultural shift, a brief summary of the evolutionary process of the SUD professional is required.

Originally, in the evolutionary process of the SUD professional role, members of Alcoholics Anonymous (that emerged in 1935) became employed in treatment facilities, and in the 1950s, professional roles for SUD counselors were created (White, 1999 as cited in Miller (2021)). Thus, the culture of the field was based on the perspective of the SUD professional having direct experience struggling with addiction themselves or having a family member with SUD. Entry into the field hinged on if the professional was "working a recovery program," not on if they had a professional degree (although some had both). The negative aspect of this culture was a closed system (i.e., the only entry into the field was if one had personal experience with addiction); in fact, those who entered the field with degrees may have been regarded with suspicion and even told by those working a recovery program to not enter the field. The positive aspect of those working a recovery program was the increased chance of viewing the client/patient with SUD through an accurate lens rather than a lens developed from their positive or negative personal/professional experiences with people with SUD.

Over time, the entry of professionals from different fields and academic training resulted in a change of the culture because they brought their expertise into the field, thereby enhancing and expanding the knowledge base of assessment and treatment. This bonus of other perspectives being helpful was accompanied by the drawback that the professionals were more unlikely to have examined their own personal/professional experiences in working with this population (Miller, 2021). This drawback potentially meant the professional had a decreased chance of viewing the client/patient with SUD through an accurate lens. This could result in a professional lens tainted by their personal/professional experiences with this population, resulting in positive or negative stereotypes of people with SUD. Canning (2021) provides numerous examples of such stereotypes.

These changes (those professionals entering the field and those professionals exiting the field) have impacted the culture of the SUD field in a couple ways. First, both the professional who is new to the field and the professional who has experience working in the field may lack mentors/colleagues who have direct experience with addiction. An example of this is where meetings consist only of those who have professional degrees and do not have experience in working directly with the SUD population as a part of their training *or* lack personal experiences related to SUD recovery. Second, in this evolving culture, there may be mistrust and suspiciousness between those SUD professionals who land in different areas on the continuum of personal experience and degrees. For example, someone who has a lot of personal experience with SUD but no professional degree may distrust a professional who has advanced degrees but lacks personal experience and vice versa.

A possible bridge between these two cultural extremes is to develop a team, a network of SUD professionals that is a combination of personal and professional SUD professionals whose positions vary on the continuum of personal experience and professional degrees. Such a blend may result in increased knowledge for both groups and enhanced assessment and treatment for the client/patient with SUD. It is important to note, however, that these professionals need to mutually trust and respect each other in order to have genuine dialogue and collaboration as they work with their SUD population. Such trust, respect, dialogue, and collaboration can result in an SUD workplace culture that places the welfare of the client as the top priority. This bridge can develop from education, supervision practices, and organizational policies and procedures for treating clients/patients with SUD.

For example, a supervisor of paraprofessionals who do not have formal training in mental health methods of confrontation may need to walk a careful balance between clients/organizations for which they work and the paraprofessionals as they discuss methods of confronting clients. The paraprofessional may not see the value of various confrontation methods because their own personal recovery involved highly intense, personal confrontation. The supervisor needs to hold the paraprofessional (who has had complaints made about them because of their highly intense, personal confrontation with clients) accountable for their behavior. At the same time, the supervisor needs to teach the paraprofessional different counseling methods of confrontation and encourage their use with clients. Such a supervisory balance may result in an "aha" experience of the paraprofessional as they realize the client is better able to hear the confrontation delivered in the new method they are using rather than the client becoming defensive in response to the highly intense, personal confrontation style.

When such network teams are not available, the professional may seek professional consultation with other SUD professionals that complement their personal/professional experience and degrees.

Note that in the following sections the author focuses on simplicity in terms of number and content of the areas presented under each of the headings. For example, in the intervention section, while there are numerous effective interventions, (e.g., evidence-based practices), only a few have been chosen: genuine counseling (Miller, 2021) and motivational interviewing (MI; Miller & Rollnick, 2013). Also, each of these interventions is only briefly described under the respective heading.

SUD Philosophy of This Book

In this section, the other section of the Miller (2024) explanation of Figure 1.1 is applied to the client with SUD:

Each cylinder represents an individual. Within each person is a parent (P), adult (A), and child (C). The internal parent guides/directs us. The internal adult is the rational, negotiating aspect of ourselves that mediates between the internal parent and the internal child. The internal child is the most vulnerable, needy, childlike aspect of ourselves. Each internal aspect (P, A, C) interacts with the other internal aspects of ourselves (P, A, or C), and these interactions can be positive or negative. (p. 73)

This chapter is now transitioning to address the objectives stated at the beginning of the chapter and will be divided into three main areas: Understanding the Active SUD Brain; Understanding What Leads to Substance Use; and Understanding Intervention Components. These three areas are based in categories that are used in Table 1.1 (e.g., the "voices of the people").

Understanding the Active SUD Brain

Because psychoactive drugs have an impact on how the brain functions, this section begins with a very basic overview of the normal functioning of the central nervous system (CNS) and how drugs impact that system and thus impact how brain components function. This section is intended to augment more extensive works on how substance use impacts the brain and its components. The reader is encouraged to read the suggested readings recommended at the end of the chapter for more additional information.

The CNS is made up of the brain and the spinal cord. This mass of nervous tissue consists of incoming sensory nervous nerves and outgoing motor nerves (Hart & Ksir, 2018). The CNS is the primary place for integration of information, learning and memory, and activity coordination (Hart & Ksir, 2018).

The following summary of how the CNS operates is based on work by Hart and Ksir (2018). In the body, tissues and organs (e.g., the brain) consist of functioning cells that interact. Because of these interactions, an organ, such as the brain, is impacted in its functioning. One cell type referred to as *neurons* (nerve cells) is primarily involved in how the brain analyzes and transmits information. The communication network in the brain operates as follows: One neuron communicates information to another (the neurotransmission process). This neurotransmission process is essentially electrical to chemical, to electrical to chemical, and so on. The communication network involves an electrical component within one neuron that has to switch to the release of chemicals (e.g., neurotransmitter) from that neuron to the next because of the gap (e.g., synaptic gap) between neurons. Specific neurotransmitters involved with the psychoactive drugs are dopamine, acetylcholine, norepinephrine, serotonin, GABA, glutamate, and endocannabinoids.

The dopamine neurotransmitter's impact on the brain has been core in the predominant theory explaining how psychoactive drugs impact brain functioning. The concept in this theory is that drug use results in addiction because drugs stimulate the sense of pleasure (reward system) in the brain. The message in the brain is "Do this (use substances) because it feels good (stimulates pleasure/reward system)."

In this predominant theory of substance use, dopamine neurons are stimulated in the brain by psychoactive drugs, and their neurotransmitter (dopamine) is involved in substance use. Essentially, drugs stimulate the sense of pleasure, the reward system, and clients with SUD keep using substances because the reward system tells the brain that the drugs are good and should be used again. However, it currently appears that other neurotransmitters (such as those mentioned at the beginning of this section) are involved in this reward system (Hart & Ksir, 2018).

It is critical to emphasize here that prolonged use of a drug impacts the brain like a switch where the person moves from using a substance to having substance use disorder. The brain now permanently operates differently, which this author refers to as the *active SUD brain* that can be found in both the client with SUD who is currently using substances and even the client with SUD in recovery who is totally abstinent. The brain is essentially changed forever for these clients with SUD.

As described previously, the brain is impacted by the use of psychoactive drugs. Three structures of the brain impacted by these drugs have been selected for emphasis here: the frontal lobe (executive functioning); the amygdala (emotional processing); and the hippocampus (memory). The *frontal lobe* is involved in decision making, problem solving, and planning—the most "human" part of the brain. The latter two structures (amygdala, hippocampus) make up the *limbic system* that is involved in emotional memory and feelings of pleasure. As psychoactive drugs impact the limbic system (amygdala, hippocampus), this more primitive brain structure overrides the frontal lobe. In summary, the behavior of a client with SUD is controlled more by the primitive brain structure (emotional processing) than the frontal lobe (executive functioning).

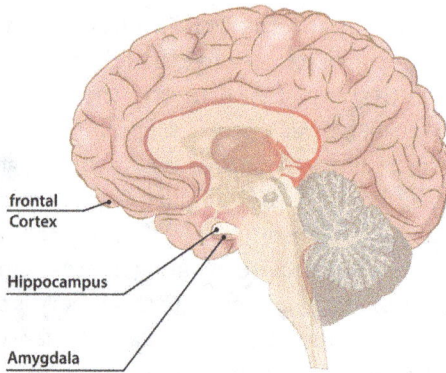

FIGURE 1.2   Frontal Lobe and Amygdala

With this basic understanding of brain functioning, the shift is to understanding the inner perspective of the client with SUD. This section describes how the active SUD brain works from the perspective of the client with SUD in order to assist the reader in understanding the inner perspective of the client with SUD. Understanding the inner perspective requires an examination of the following: view of the world, meaning of the world, and hallmark of addiction.

View of the World

It is necessary to understand how clients with SUD who are actively using and those in recovery view the world differently. Basically, the frontal lobe is inhibited in its functioning because of a "double negative": The substance "tells" the frontal lobe (the part of our brains that

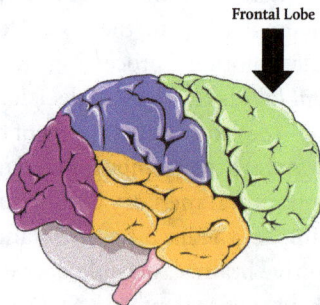

FIGURE 1.3   Frontal Lobe

tells us to "be quiet") to be quiet. The result is decreased reasoning controls in the client with SUD. The client with SUD who is in recovery may also experience this decreased reasoning.

The impact on the limbic system may result in some clients with SUD describing a heightened sensitivity to emotions and having an "emotional memory from hell." The author refers to this as the "flying amygdala," where the emotions of a client with SUD are exaggerated and out of control. Clients with SUD generally view the world through an extreme "emotional memory lens" that may be a result of both substance use and trauma experiences (e.g., various forms of violence, such as war, childhood sexual abuse, etc.). This change in the brain's limbic system can be present even into their SUD recovery, resulting in decreased emotional controls that make the SUD population difficult to work with professionally.

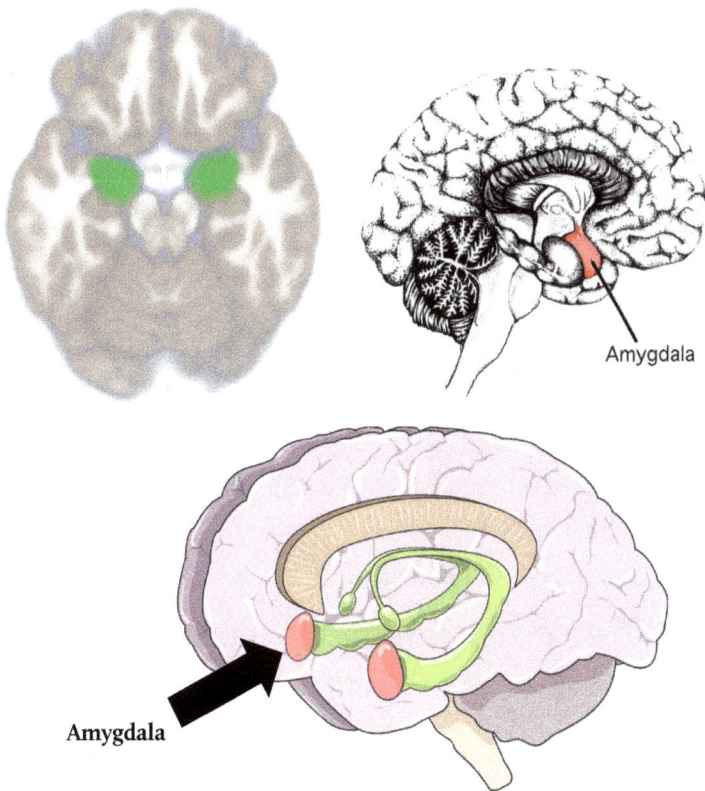

FIGURE 1.4 Amygdala

For example, a client with SUD may verbally attack the helping professional who has approached them in a calm, supportive, welcoming manner by calling them names or unjustifiably accusing them of disrespectful behaviors. This author believes that such an attack is the result of the substance use culture in which they obtained their substances (e.g., "Do not trust anyone") as well as the impact of their previous experiences trauma (prior to or during their substance use) resulting in kindness "being a stranger" to them. The helping professional may think of these interactions metaphorically: They are a stranger approaching a wounded animal in the bushes who is both frightened and wary of strangers—even helpful, kind ones.

Meaning of the World

The client with SUD, through their substance use, has become narrowly focused on the substance as the solution that fixes everything. The substance is seen as a blanket solution to all their life problems, and as their SUD develops, they increasingly commit their time, energy, and money to obtaining that blanket solution. Their meaning of the world has become a narrow focus (Miller, 2021).

Hallmark of Addiction

The two previous aspects—how the client with SUD t views the world and how they make meaning of the world—result in the "hallmark of addiction": continued use in spite of negative consequences. The helping professional who is mystified by how their client continues to use in spite of negative consequences (e.g., a woman who values her children has them removed legitimately by child protective services due to her use of substances) is witnessing how they view the world and make meaning of it.

BOX 1B: HALLMARK OF ADDICTION

Continued use in spite of negative consequences.

Through their use of substances, their client has also developed poor impulse control (e.g., "I want what I want when I want it—NOW!").

BOX 1C: POOR IMPULSE CONTROL

I want what I want
when I want it!
NOW!

The client with SUD will use "Teflon defenses" of denial, where they are blameless for their use, and *projection*, where others are blamed for their use (Miller, 2021). Note that Teflon was once used as a manufactured coating to items such as cookware that allowed ingredients (e.g., fried eggs) to slide off the cookware easily. That is why the author calls them "Teflon defenses" because they allow for feedback from others to "slide off" of the SUD person.

BOX 1D: TEFLON DEFENSES

Denial
&
Projection

They are experiencing the "disease of isolation" where there is a complicated relationship between the reality that they "can't" change (i.e., they are powerless over the disease) and they "won't" change (i.e., they are protecting their supply and their pattern of use). The helping professional can approach this complicated relationship through the intervention of compassionate accountability presented later in this chapter's section of interventions.

Understanding What Leads to Substance Use

Miller (2021) summarizes the biopsychosocial model—written here as the BioPsychoSocial model to emphasize the different components of the model: *Bio* (e.g., genetics), *Psycho* (psyche-self, or what is inside the person; e.g., personality traits), and *Social* (what is outside

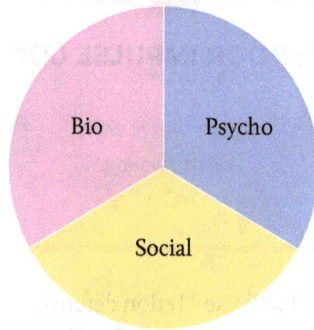

FIGURE 1.5   Biopsychosocial Model, Part 1

the person; e.g., trauma, family, cultural issues), with especially the psycho and social components increasingly interacting as the substance use continues.

It is a flexible model that looks at each individual differently. It can be thought of metaphorically as each client with SUD being like a pie that is sliced differently. While the *Bio* component may change in size from one person to another (e.g., one person may have more of a genetic predisposition than another), the *Psycho* and *Social* components may vary in size due to both differences within each person (*Psycho*) as well as their unique *Social* experiences. These 2 areas (*Psycho*, *Social*) interact and influence each other as noted in Figures 1.6 and 1.9. For example, a very sensitive person (*Psycho* factor) may experience the same negative *Social* experiences in high school as another SUD person, however, due to their heightened sensitivity,

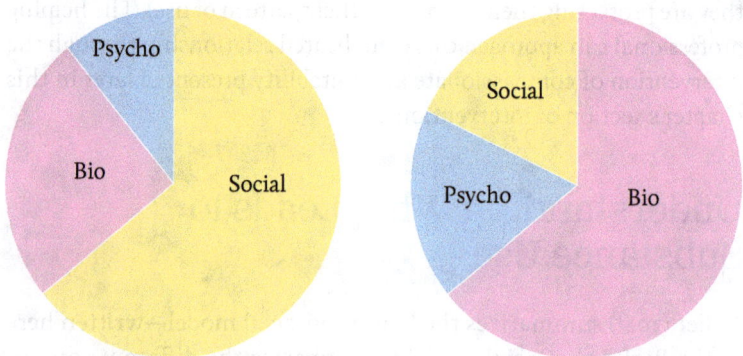

FIGURE 1.6   Biopsychosocial Model, Part 2

they have a stronger influencing interaction between their *Psycho* and *Social* components.

The story of substance use of each client with SUD needs to be examined carefully for how the components of this model are divided for their unique distribution of interacting, contributing factors that have led to their SUD as well as maintaining their use and contributing to their struggles in their recovery. For example, in the interaction of the psycho and social components, clients with SUD may tend to want to please others, manipulate the world for their own benefit, and have high expectations of themselves and others. They may also struggle with emotions of shame, anger, and unresolved grief that are related to their trauma of both abuse and neglect. Such examination can assist both the helping professional and the client develop compassion for how the substance use began and the development of the SUD.

Understanding Intervention Components

Prior to the discussion of intervention components, specific factors impacting the professional—and thus client care—are reviewed here. First, increased use of technology and a growing emphasis of provider networks on efficiency, money, and accountability may result in a dehumanization of both the professional, their client, and the quality of the therapeutic relationship. The impact of these influencing factors, in combination with the cultural shift discussed previously, can result in reduction of:

- recovering individuals in the field
- quality supervision time
- staff meetings where clinical issues are raised
- time to reflect on clinical issues

Second, those in the workforce may experience an increase in stress resulting in a decreased interest in learning. For example, they may attend online trainings (rather than in-person ones) because it saves themselves or the agency they work for time, energy, and money. As a result, their attendance may not be as closely monitored and they lose the "3D" opportunities to (a) view demonstration of clinical techniques, network with other professionals, and find mentors beyond their workplace. There may be more emphasis on knowledge than skill acquisition (e.g., to pass a licensure exam).

As stated previously, these forces can impact the quality of the therapeutic relationship. The personal self-reflection questions in Box 1E may assist the counselor in examining their current philosophical status in the field.

BOX 1E: PERSONAL SELF-REFLECTION QUESTIONS

1. What is my view of clients with SUD?
2. What is my motivation for doing this work?
3. What/who sustains me in this work?
4. What gives me hope for change in my clients with SUD?
5. What are reliable sources of information for my SUD work?

HOW

The helping professional can answer the question "How can I do this work?" with the acronym of **HOW**: Be Honest, Open, and Willing. HOW can be a guide to establishing a genuine dialogue between helping professionals and their clients. Such a dialogue creates an interactive exchange of information that invites a hope for change in the client with SUD: "I can talk with this person honestly about my struggles." Note that this acronym can be useful to the client with SUD when they are wondering how to do something.

Compassionate Accountability

Compassionate accountability (Miller, 2021) is a critical intervention with clients with SUD because, as stated earlier, they need both compassion and accountability from the helping professional in order to cease their destructive SUD-related behavior and maintain such a change. This *compassionate accountability* means that the professional finds a balance between compassion for the client's story of what led to the substance use while also holding them accountable for their SUD-related behavior. For example, in a calm, nonjudgmental manner, the helping professional presents a diagnosis to a client in a language they understand. Special treatment of the client with SUD (too much compassion for their story *or* too high of accountability) is avoided, and the client with SUD receives treatment that best meets the welfare of the client. This compassionate accountability is an excellent companion to motivational interviewing (Miller & Rollnick, 2013).

Motivational Interviewing

In particular, this confrontation style of motivational interviewing places the struggle of change (e.g., to use substances vs. to not use substances) *within* the client rather than *between* the helping professional and the client. This is a very effective style of breaking through the Teflon defenses discussed earlier because the client is being asked to examine their ambivalence to change, which requires them examining their denial and projection as the helping professional asks them for clarifying information about their ambivalence in a spirit of compassionate accountability. They are needing to explain the discrepancy in their behaviors: their values versus their actual behavior.

Recovery Communities

The genuine therapeutic relationship is mimicking what needs to be replicated in the life of the client with SUD. In order to begin and maintain a change in relation to their SUD, they need to have the professional assist them in creating communities of compassionate accountability that replicate the therapeutic relationship in terms of genuineness, honesty, respect, and care. Such replication can result in recovery communities where compassionate accountability is as core as it is in the helping relationship with the same recovery benefits. By spending time in community with others who share similar SUD struggles, care about them, and honestly and directly confront them, the client with SUD can learn more about themselves and how they interact with others interpersonally.

Such confrontation can occur directly as well as indirectly in group counseling or self-help groups. This confrontation is necessary for the client with SUD who may be used to creating an image that is convincing to others. A community of others who struggle with a similar SUD and know the client is immensely beneficial to the client because "You can't con a con artist." Whereas the client with SUD may be able to create an image to one individual (e.g., sole helping professional), they are unable to do so when in a recovering community setting; they cannot create a false image of who they are with an entire community.

Direct confrontation of the client with SUD can occur in group counseling through feedback shared with the client by the leader and group counseling members (Miller, 2021). The indirect confrontation of the issues of the client with SUD in group counseling may occur as the client hears the recovery stories of other group counseling members and watches them address their issues in the group.

By contrast, self-help group confrontation of the client with SUD may be a "flip" of the emphasis in group counseling. In this setting, indirect confrontation of the issues of the client with SUD may occur as the client hears the recovery stories of other self-help group members and watches them address their issues in the group. Direct confrontation of the client with SUD can occur in self-help groups through related aspects of self-help group, such as sponsorship (i.e., someone chosen by the client who has been in recovery longer than them and individually mentors them outside the self-help group meeting).

These communities (e.g., group counseling; self-help groups) are places "bigger than self" that can assist clients with SUD in several ways:

- These communities help clients move from the "back of the brain" (e.g., amygdala) to the "front of the brain" (e.g., frontal lobe), as described by some clients in recovery (e.g., "I hear the ridiculousness of my idea/plan by hearing myself say it out loud").
- They provide meaning because clients feel needed and wanted by others.
- They help clients avoid "switching" to another SUD (e.g., gambling) or extreme habitual patterns of behavior (e.g., shopping, sex).
- They can teach clients how to self-soothe (e.g., calm themselves down) and choose behaviors that are not based in fear.

Overall, they are developing a "teeter-totter" of a balanced lifestyle where they learn in these recovery communities how to "live life on life's terms" while "insisting on enjoying life"—a life that is anchored in serenity and hope. The teeter-totter consists of the fulcrum being the recovery community, with serenity on one end of the teeter-totter and hope on the other.

Serenity   Hope

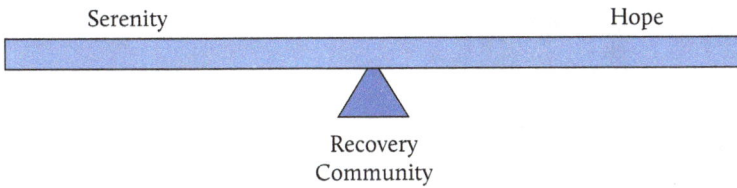

Recovery
Community

The Teeter-Totter of a Balanced Lifestyle

FIGURE 1.7   The Teeter-Totter of a Balanced Lifestyle

However, the BioPsychoSocial model is revisited here because it is also useful in the choice of the helping professional's intervention approaches. The overall intervention involves the *Bio* (e.g., medical needs), *Psycho* (e.g., personality traits), and *Social* (what is outside the person; e.g., trauma, family, cultural issues) with, once again, all areas interacting with an emphasis on the interaction of the psycho and social components.

The flexibility of the model allows the helping professional to look at each individual's treatment interventions differently. Again, the model can be thought of metaphorically as each client's interventions being like a pie that is sliced differently.

Some clients may require more *Bio* interventions than *Psycho* or *Social* interventions, while other client may require more *Psycho* or *S ocial* interventions than *Bio* interventions. Health care professionals can use this model in the choice of an "intervention package" that best suites the welfare of the client. For example, a client with opioid

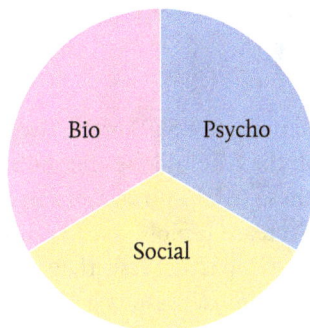

FIGURE 1.8   Biopsychosocial
Model, Part 1 (repeated)

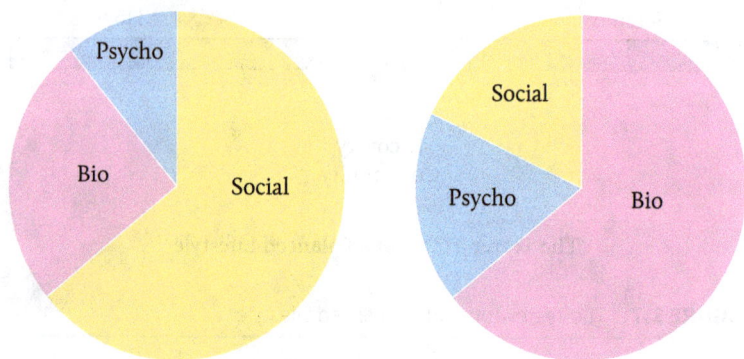

FIGURE 1.9   Biopsychosocial Model, Part 2 (repeated)

addiction may need more medical interventions (*Bio*) than a client with SUD who is open to self-reflection and responds well to individual assistance from the helping professional (*Psycho*) or the client who needs more of a recovering community (*Social*).

SUMMARY

This chapter has presented information on three critical areas in facilitating SUD recovery: how the active SUD brain operates; what leads to substance use; and intervention components that hinge of the importance of the therapeutic alliance established between the helping professional and the client with SUD.

KEY POINTS

1. To understand the active SUD brain, two sections of the brain were explored: the frontal lobe and the amygdala. Substance use changes these two brain sections in decreased reasoning controls and decreased emotional controls, respectively, in the client with SUD, impacting how they see and make meaning in the world. This impact results in the hallmark of addiction: continued use in spite of negative consequence.

2. To enhance the understanding of what leads to substance use, the BioPsychoSocial model was examined where each

client with SUD is viewed metaphorically as a "pie" with the components (e.g., bio, psycho, social) divided uniquely. This careful, individualized assessment of the contributing factors to substance use is needed to facilitate the recovery from the SUD.

3. In order to understand facilitating the presence or the recovering SUD brain necessary for SUD recovery, the importance of a real, genuine, caring, and honest relationship between the helping professional and the client with SUD was explored. This relationship is based on the helping professional listening without judgment, holding the client with compassionate accountability, and setting up recovery communities with the client using the BioPsychoSocial model as a guide.

Just as despair can come to one only from other human beings, hope too can be given to one only by other human beings.

—Elie Wiesel

INTERACTIVE READER COMPONENTS

Case Study 1.1

Your client is asked to provide a urine specimen on a regularly scheduled basis as a part of their treatment program to hold them accountable for their behavior (e.g., their usage). Your client provides the urine specimen on the scheduled date; however, the lab accidently contaminates the sample, and you need to ask the client to provide another specimen. Your client becomes incredibly angry at the request to provide another specimen, stating, "I already gave one on the date it was scheduled, and now you are asking me to give another on an unscheduled date. I should NOT be asked to do this." You remain caring and calm as you inform your client that they need to provide another specimen. Your client tests positive for drug use. When confronted by you in a gentle, calm, but firm manner that focuses on the lab results, your client admits they had been strategically detoxing from drugs before scheduled tests, and you discuss your client's ambivalence with being abstinent from alcohol/drugs.

How does this interaction reflect the "Responses of Hopeful Information" section in Table 1.1?

- Their narrow focus of how they see the world and the hallmark of addiction
- Compassionate accountability
- Protecting their supply (WON'T change)
- Disease of addiction (CAN'T change)

Case Study 1.2

Imagine you are working with a client with SUD who is planning to use substances. As you work with this person:

1. How would you explain the active SUD brain (e.g., frontal lobe, amygdala) in terms of how they view the world and make meaning of it?
2. How would you explain the related concepts (e.g., the hallmark of addiction, poor impulse control, and Teflon defenses)?

Exercise 1.1

Use Figure 1.1 as you respond to these questions about working with the same client with SUD presented in Case Study 1.2:

1. How would you explain the concepts of parent (P), **a**dult (A), and child (C) with regard to their substance use?
2. How would you explain the positive interactions between the three components that lead to avoidance of active substance abuse?

Example of positive interactive dialogue between the three components:

The P says: "Do NOT use substances. They only cause you problems."

The **C** replies: "I WANT WHAT I WANT WHEN I WANT IT—NOW!"

The A says: "Let's call someone who will help figure out how to work out this conflict between P and C that helps avoid substance abuse."

The C says to the P and A: "Okay." (and avoids substance use)

3. How would you explain the negative interactions between the three components that lead to active substance abuse?

    Example of negative interactive dialogue between the three components:

    The P says: "Do NOT use substances. They only cause you problems."

    The **C** replies: "I WANT WHAT I WANT WHEN I WANT IT—NOW!"

    The A says: "Let's call someone who will help figure out how to work out this conflict between P and C that helps avoid substance abuse."

    The C says to the P and A: "SHUT UP!" (and resumes substance abuse)

Exercise 1.2

Use Figures 1.5 and 1.8 to guide you on how you would divide the Bio-PsychoSocial components with the same client with SUD presented in Case Study 1.2.

Exercise 1.3

With the BioPsychoSocial components you outlined in Exercise 1.2 for your client, use the following intervention components:

- HOW (honest, open, willing)
- Compassionate accountability
- Motivational interviewing
- Recovery communities

SUGGESTED READINGS

Readings (Substance Use Impact on the Brain)

Hart, C. H., & Ksir, C. J. (2018). *Drugs, society, and human behavior* (18th ed.). McGraw Hill.

> This book consists of 18 chapters. One section in particular ("How Drugs Work") has two relevant chapters: "The Nervous System" and "The Actions of Drugs."

Readings (Related Topics)

Canning, P. (2021). *Killing season: A paramedic's dispatches from the front lines of the opioid epidemic.* John Hopkins University Press.

> This book has 29 chapters. The emphasis of the book is on harm reduction approaches in addressing the opioid epidemic through the author's eyewitness experiences of addiction and overdose. It is interspersed with stories about individuals with SUD and their loved ones that pierce stereotypes of those individuals. It also critiques policies that contribute to the opioid epidemic.

RESOURCES/WEBSITES

National Institute on Alcohol Abuse and Alcoholism (NIAAA)
   https://www.niaaa.nih.gov
National Institute on Drug Abuse (NIDA)
   https://www.drugabuse.gov
Substance Abuse and Mental Health Services Administration (SAMHSA)
   https://www.samhsa.gov

Credits

COLLOQUIAL EXPRESSIONS IN THE SUBSTANCE USE DISORDER RECOVERY COMMUNITY

OBJECTIVES*

1. Further enhance the integration of both the knowledge and experience of paraprofessionals and professionals, as discussed in Chapter 1, through the use of colloquial expressions of the SUD recovery community (e.g., AA).

2. Learn the concepts of emotional sobriety to assist the person with SUD in their recovery.

3. Increase knowledge and application of the recovery communities of group counseling and self-help groups that help individuals with SUD develop a balanced lifestyle of serenity and hope.

*Note that these objectives overlap in their concepts and their use of AA colloquial expressions that provide a framework for understanding the concepts.

Overview of the Chapter

In the Chapter 1 overview, the concept of Americans' confusion about substance use was presented. This confusion results from conflicting information they receive from the areas of public policy, public interest, overdose death statistics, and substance use statistics. There is also discussion in the chapter of the SUD field's cultural transition that stems from current SUD professionals ranging in both their experience with addiction (e.g., "working a recovery program") and their professional training. Both may impact the "lens" through which they view the person with SUD whom they treat and their treatment and referral processes of the person with SUD.

Because of the author's belief that SUD recovery communities are needed in order for the client with SUD to live a balanced lifestyle of serenity and hope, two communities (group counseling and self-help groups) that practice "compassionate accountability" are explored in this chapter. Both of these communities are an expansion of the reader's compassionate accountability relationship with the client with SUD discussed in Chapter 1 and shown in the Image 2.1 of the author with a mock client.

Image 2.1

These communities are presented following a discussion of the potential of a stigmatic lens that can impact (a) the view of the client with SUD, (b) the treatment and referral process of the client with SUD, and (c) the recovery process of the client with SUD. An understanding of the stigma of surrounding SUD is necessary here because the recovery communities can assist the client with SUD in living with the stigma because they also experience it.

Potential for a "Stigmatic Lens"

The potential for a "stigmatic lens" through which the American public and SUD professionals may view the person with SUD is best described by Moyers (2006) in his book *Broken: My Story of Addiction and Redemption*. In this book, Moyers highlights the stigma of addiction by making the following statements as he shares his personal story of having two chronic diseases (cancer and alcohol/drug addiction):

> When my doctor told me I had cancer, he didn't raise his eyebrows or wag his finger at me. ... Nobody was to

blame—I just happened to get it, and when I did, everyone stepped in to help. During the diagnosis, treatment, and recovery stages of my cancer, I was overwhelmed by offers of sympathy and support from family, friends, and even strangers. ...

It was a completely different story with my addiction. ... *What's wrong with you?* [was the reaction of others to the addiction] and that sentiment was secretly shared by everyone, including me. ... Why couldn't I just exert some willpower and strength of character and stop this self-destructive behavior? (Moyers, 2006, pp. 337, 339–340)

He then broadens the scope from his personal experiences of being stigmatized for having an SUD: "Public attitudes toward the victims of these diseases are as different as night and day" (Moyers, 2006, p. 337). Moyers (2006) describes "deep-seated prejudices and misconceptions that alcoholics and other drug-addicted people [experience]" (p. 317), such as (a) they are weak-willed, lack self-discipline, lack moral virtue; (b) they have character disorders, psychological problems, social problems; and (c) they don't respond to treatment.

Moyers (2006) goes on to state, "Every addicted and recovering person has felt the sting of stigma either publicly or privately." (p. 322). In summary, Moyers (2006) says, "addiction is unlike cancer or any other chronic progressive disease in the world" (p. 343) in terms of how it operates in the person (as reflected in the excerpted questions column of Table 1.1). Due to the stigma of addiction, it is treated differently by others.

Questions asked regarding specific topics

- Why do they use substances?
- Why don't they see themselves as addicted?
- How can a substance be so consuming that they give up their lives for it?
- Why is it so hard for them to stop?
- What is the "wake-up call"?
- What is the "trigger(s)" to waking up?
- When does a person have enough?
- How long do you wait for them to change/get sober?
- How many chances do you give them to sober up before you give up?

I end this section with three suggestions for you, the reader, to consider:

1. Recall the stigmatizing descriptions regarding individuals with SUD you heard/witnessed personally and/or professionally.
2. Evaluate the stigmatizing treatment of individuals with SUD you heard/witnessed personally and/or professionally.
3. Find the similarities of chronic, progressive diseases, including addiction.

The stress management tip for this chapter in Box 2A reflects the importance of community for the professional also.

BOX 2A: STRESS MANAGEMENT TIP

Complete the blank

I feel safe at school/work in these physical spaces (e.g., classroom/office, break room):

_____.

I feel supported at school/work by these people:

_____.

The barriers to my feeling safe/supported in terms of my time, energy, and money are:

_____.

I can work around these barriers by:

_____.

Recovery Story

I found I had come home, at last, to my own kind.

(Alcoholics Anonymous, 1976, p. 228)

The Story Behind the Statement

A bright, charismatic, handsome, long-haired, middle-aged man was arrested by federal agents in his home for dealing drugs and placed in a county federal jail for less than one year as he awaited trial. This arrest/jail incarceration physically separated him from the alcohol and drugs that had consumed him for over 3 decades. During the last decade of his use, he was a major drug dealer. Incarceration provided him with time to reflect on his life, and he began to think he might have a problem with alcohol and drugs. Because he was a federal jail inmate, he was not allowed to attend Alcoholics Anonymous (AA) meetings because the meetings were held in an insecure area of the county jail. His cellmate, who was experienced in being incarcerated, wanted to help him survive incarceration because he had never been jailed before. In an authoritative manner, his cellmate made suggestions to him on surviving incarceration. One of the suggestions was that he attend the jail's weekly chapel meeting. He was hesitant to attend the meeting even though the only positive experiences in his life had happened when he was young and attended a Judeo-Christian church with his loving, middle-class family. Given his positive family and life experiences, he did not understand why he had never been "comfortable in his own skin" or felt like he was "good enough." Then, when he was a young, married man with one child, a close family member committed suicide without explanation (e.g., did not leave a note or present any indicators of suicide). This trauma caused him to turn his back on his religion and God.

Early in his incarceration, he decided to follow his cellmate's directive to attend the worship service. Much to his surprise, the first time he attended the service, he had a spiritual experience and responded to the altar call at the end of the service where worshippers came forward to accept Jesus into their life. As he walked to and then kneeled at the altar, he felt like the "weight of the world had been lifted from his shoulders." When the service ended, he accepted the minister's gift of a Bible and heard his encouragement to start a weekly Bible study group in the jail. He began a

Bible study group shortly after this spiritual experience and led/became a part of a supportive jail community that gave him serenity, hope, and life meaning throughout his incarceration. One week after he was transferred to a federal prison, he advocated for himself to be able to attend prison AA meetings. In those meetings, he met men like himself who were able to both talk about the tragedy of their lives and laugh together about life. He had not laughed in years. He wanted what they had: They knew what was important in life but were able to laugh at life even in prison. He felt as though he had come home to a community of people like himself who were supportive and nurturing of each other. He wanted to be a part of this community because he saw genuine concern and caring for him in their eyes.

As he stayed in that AA community, he realized that he had been given a gift of sobriety and that he had to both change who he was, with the support of his AA community, and paradoxically, in order to keep this gift of sobriety, he had to carry the message of hope to other alcoholics (the 12th step) through being of service to others (e.g., responding to another alcoholic's request for help to get sober). Through both his religious and AA communities, he realized he never had to be lonely or use alcohol/drugs again. He was successful at staying sober, without relapse, for over 3 decades.

Author Personal Reflections

The opening statement for this chapter expresses one recovering alcoholic's view of the Alcoholics Anonymous community. The statement and the following "true story" highlight the importance of community in the recovery process of the client with SUD. A supportive community is critical for the client with SUD as they live with the philosophy of a little "i" within a BIG "WE." This means that the individual examines their thoughts, feelings, and behaviors in their recovery process, making responsible choices that are respectful of themselves and others. A *BIG "WE"* reflects the importance of community in the recovery of the client with SUD that assists them in making responsible choices by sharing stories of hope from their life struggles with substances and supporting the individual in making responsible behavioral choices in the context of their individual life circumstances. In healthy recovery communities, people can know about an individual's flaws but still care deeply about them and give them "room to be" both in terms of their flaws and their strengths. I have sometimes heard people express envy of the healthy recovery community of a client with SUD, wishing they, as a person without SUD, had such a community. I have gently responded to their envy by saying, "They have paid a high admission ticket into that community."

In response to the stories of long-term recovery throughout this book, such as the one above, it has always surprised me that people (e.g., lay, professional) have a tendency to say to individuals in long-term recovery, "Are you *still* going to those meetings (e.g., Alcoholics Anonymous) after all these years?" I believe my surprise is because I never hear people say to individuals who go to other communities such as church for support, "Are you *still* going to church after all these years?" As described in the story above, individuals with long-term recovery may still attend meetings after many years for support and guidance that they need as they live their lives.

The Resources/Websites section at the end of this chapter notes some of the various groups (e.g., recovery communities) available to the client with SUD: 12-step self-help groups; abstinence-based self-help groups that are spirituality specific, and harm reduction groups. I have chosen to focus on only one group, Alcoholics Anonymous (AA). My rationale for this choice was that this original self-help group (i.e., recovery community) is the one most commonly known self-help group among both professional and lay people. The reader is encouraged to view the examination of this organization as a prototype for other recovery communities and "translate" the underlying concepts of AA to other recovery communities that they believe best serve their clients with SUD. In addition to abstinence-based recovery communities, harm reduction support groups have been included in response to the United States' growing interest in this philosophy as a result of the current opioid epidemic in this country. Note, however, that AA has as its requirement for membership simply that the individual has a desire to stop drinking, not that they make a commitment to abstinence. Therefore, this author believes this organization has at its core a harm reduction focus.

I will also present suggested guidelines to the reader on assisting their clients with SUD on the choice of recovery communities available to them. These guidelines are necessary because of the variability of individual groups in terms of their health (e.g., healthy and unhealthy groups), the interest and motivation of individual clients with SUD, and the use of various aspects of the recovery community supports (e.g., sponsor, level of community involvement) of individual clients with SUD. Whatever choice of community is made by the client with SUD, I encourage the reader to approach the client with two questions that are critical to the recovery of the client with SUD:

- "To what lengths are you willing to go to reduce the harm that substances are causing your life?"
- "How much do you want this change?"

These two questions require the client with SUD to carefully examine the lengths they are willing to go to in order to reduce the harm of the substances—the time, energy, and money they are willing to commit to the change needed. Is it the same level of commitment they made to obtain their mood-altering substances? If so, they will need a community of support on which to draw because it is too hard to do alone. These questions can be used repeatedly by the health professional throughout the recovery process of the client with SUD.

My hope is that the reader, as noted in Chapter 1, will continue to read this chapter with a critical eye, choosing only those aspects of the chapter that match them and their clients as they work to serve the best interest of their clients. An additional caution to the reader is that some of the excerpts from the AA literature have strong religious terms, such as "God."

Integration of the Knowledge and Experience of Paraprofessionals and Professionals

Integrating the knowledge and experience of paraprofessionals and professionals is an important consideration in working with an SUD population. To facilitate this integration, a discussion of the "professional lens" and an "addictionary" follows.

Professional Lens

The professional lens discussed in Chapter 1 may be impacted positively or negatively by the professional's personal/professional experiences with an SUD population. The potential for a stigmatic lens, as highlighted by Moyers's (2006) experiences, may be explained by two factors contributing to greater compassion for cancer patients than patients with SUD.

FACTOR 1: DIFFERENT VIEW OF CHRONIC, PROGRESSIVE DISEASES

Some people may have the view "No one has control over cancer so no one is to blame for getting it, but individuals have control over becoming addicted so it is their fault." When this view is mixed with the knowledge that addiction is a disease (like cancer), the client with SUD may receive a double message from others (including professionals). While verbally the client receives information it is a disease, they may also receive underlying nonverbal and verbal messages that are experienced as a moral judgment. For example, in sharp contrast with the patient with cancer, the client with SUD receives information about treatment options, but they are spoken in a tone that communicates blame on the client with SUD and that their condition is hopeless in terms of recovery.

There are possible remedies for the elimination of the double message:

- At a young age or early in their professional SUD career, individuals receive information that is consistent with the view of addiction as a disease.
- When individuals experience confusion on how to view an SUD, they are encouraged to switch it (the SUD) to another disease (cancer) to have a clearer lens that eliminates negative moral judgment. For example, a patient with cancer would probably never hear (or pick up in an underlying message) "We are not going to treat your cancer because it is hopeless; it will return no matter what we do." However, a client with SUD may receive a similar message from others: "We will treat your SUD, but it is hopeless and your SUD will return no matter what we do." This may be especially true for clients with SUD who have a history of relapse following treatment, whereas patients with cancer who have had unsuccessful treatments of their cancer may receive a message that different treatments will be tried until a successful one is found and that they are not to blame for its reoccurrence.

FACTOR 2: OFFENSIVE BEHAVIORS

Using Moyers's (2006) terminology, others may have experienced "monstrous" behaviors from the client with SUD in the throes of an active SUD. Such behaviors may result in different amounts of compassion felt toward the patient with cancer versus the client with SUD. While both patients with cancer and clients with SUD may have offensive behaviors as a result of their disease, the difference in compassion may be due to increased frequency, intensity, and focused harm of the behavior of the client with SUD as experienced by others. Also, the client with SUD may interact with others unpredictably, adding another dimension of confusion and fear in those around them; no one can predict how the client with an active SUD may interact with them. For example, a patient with cancer may sometimes be curt or rude to their child (mild intensity, focused harmful behavior) when personally experiencing powerlessness in relation to their cancer. A client with SUD may physically explode and abuse their child (extreme intensity; focused harmful behavior) when experiencing powerlessness during their active SUD. While both cancer and SUD have a similar disease process, the increased frequency, intensity, and focused harm of the SUD-related behavior requires a more urgent accountability of the behavior. Unlike cancer, the more severe SUD-related behavior complicates the view of SUD as a disease.

Finally, offensive behaviors of the client with SUD can continue into their recovery if they are unable to find a balanced lifestyle, as discussed in the following sections on emotional sobriety and SUD recovery communities (e.g., group counseling, self-help groups). Without emotional sobriety and SUD recovery communities, the individuals in their lives experience unstable and unpredictable behavior of the client with SUD.

The Integrating Bridge of the Addictionary

Because the culture of the SUD field has changed as a result of the varied personal and professional experiences of SUD professionals, this section will blend the "insider knowledge and experience" (para-professionals) with the "outsider knowledge" (professional training) through the use of an "addictionary" based on colloquial expressions of the SUD recovery community of Alcoholics Anonymous (AA). The reader is encouraged to remember that colloquial terms and phrases may vary due to time, location, and SUD population and is advised to ask the client with SUD what they mean when they use a term unfamiliar to the professional. Such a request conveys a genuine curiosity and honesty to the client that, in the author's experience, is typically met with the client being eager to educate the professional.

The term "addictionary" has been used previously as a proposal requesting more precise terminology in the SUD field (e.g., misuse, abuse, dependence; Kelly, 2004) and later as "addiction-ary" to encourage agreed terminology to reduce stigma and discrimination in policies of a public health and social nature (Kelly et al., 2016). Here the term is used because of the integration of insider knowledge and experience with outsider knowledge. The addictionary terms and phrases will be interwoven throughout the following three sections as well as in Appendices 2A (drug terms) and 2B (drug-related terms), which contain short lists of drug terms/drug-related terms and their definitions. It was developed by the author in collaboration with three SUD professionals as noted above the Appendices section. The reader is encouraged to read Appendix 2A and Appendix 2B as examples if they decide to develop their own list of terms for their respective SUD population and to consult texts, such as Hart and Ksir (2018), for explanation of drug actions on the neurotransmission process.

Addictionary terms and phrases can assist the helping professional in developing supportive recovery communities (e.g., group counseling, self-help groups) for the client with SUD because of being based on colloquial expressions of both "street culture" and the SUD recovery community of Alcoholics Anonymous (AA). The addictionary assists the helping professional in "learning the language" of SUD counseling (insider knowledge and experience) that facilitates finding the best referral, the best match, of the client with SUD with these supportive recovery communities. These supportive recovery communities are necessary to recovery because a good match between the client with SUD and the community can assist them in obtaining and maintaining a balanced lifestyle of serenity and hope through compassionate accountability: compassion for their story while holding them accountable for their behavior. Specific suggestions on referrals to group counseling and self-help groups will be housed in the final section of the chapter, as well as suggestions on how the helping professional can enhance their knowledge and experience of the mental health culture of these groups.

While addictionary terms and phrases are drawn from the specific group of Alcoholics Anonymous, to assist the reader in making the best referral possible to an AA group, depending on the term and phrase, they may also be used in a referral process to other self-help groups. At the core of referrals to 12-step meetings, such as AA, are three changes required of the client with SUD in order for them to stay sober. The following three changes, as noted in bold, make up the standard AA recovery formula. They are accompanied by AA slogans in parentheses. The three changes the client with SUD needs to make are:

- **Change their behavior** ("Don't drink or use drugs").
- **Avoid isolation** ("Go to meetings").
- **Read philosophical materials that support recovery** ("Read the Big Book," the main AA text; Alcoholics Anonymous, 1976). See Box 2B.

BOX 2B: AA BIG BOOK

Nickname Oral History

The "Big Book" is the nickname for the main text *Alcoholics Anonymous* (1976) of the organization of Alcoholics Anonymous (AA).

The oral history of AA is that the book received its nickname because it was a big book.

Content

The book contains a theory of alcoholism and the 12 steps in the first section of 164 pages, and the remaining pages of the second section consist of stories of people with alcohol use disorder. The length and content of the second section depends on the edition of the text.

Asking follow-up questions beyond "Did you go to a meeting?" (e.g., "What was it like for you to attend the meeting?" "How were you received by the group?") enhances the quality of the match of the client with SUD with the AA group. Such processing is expanded on later in this chapter.

This same three-part formula and follow-up questions can be applied to all the groups (e.g., 12-step groups, harm reduction groups) found in the Resources and Websites section at the end of the chapter.

In summary, as stated in Chapter 1, the relationship between the helping professional and the client with SUD is critical to the conveyance of helpful information whether one is an "insider" or an "outsider." What is necessary is the creation of a safe place where the following can be discussed in the client's language, as shown in the samples provided in the appendices:

- Drug Terms (Appendix 2A)
- Drug-Related Terms: Process and Impact (Appendix 2B)
- Drug-Related Terms: People and Locations (Appendix 2B)

The next section explores the concept of emotional sobriety. This concept overlaps with the integration of the knowledge and experience of paraprofessionals and professionals because the client with SUD needs to face their life circumstances with balance and maturity (i.e., emotional sobriety). While having a close connection with the AA community, the emotional sobriety concept also applies to other self-help groups.

Emotional Sobriety

Emotional sobriety is a concept that is helpful to an SUD person in recovery. In this section, the definition of the concept by Bill Wilson, one of the co-founders of AA, as well as others' definitions are presented here.

Bill Wilson's Introduction of the Term

Bill Wilson (otherwise known as "Bill W."), one of the two cofounders of AA (the other was Dr. Bob), introduced the concept of emotional sobriety when he wrote a letter for the publication of the *AA Grapevine* in 1958 (Wilson, 1958). In this personal letter about his own recovery process where he shared his struggles with depression and grief, he shared his realization that he had struggled since his adolescence with "those adolescent urges so many of us have for top approval, perfect security, and perfect romance" (Wilson, 1958, p. 1). He described himself as "unable to get off the emotional merry-go-round" (Wilson, 1958, p. 1) because of a basic flaw of his of dependence on people or circumstances to meet those adolescent needs for prestige and security. It was this dependence that led to demands to possess and control others and his circumstances with the hope he would feel better about himself and achieve/meet those needs. He worked the 12 steps of AA (see Box 2C below) that focused on care of both self and others as well as service to others. In AA terms, he followed the philosophy:

- "Love and tolerance is our code. And we have ceased fighting anything or anyone-even alcohol" (Alcoholics Anonymous, 1976, p. 84). "The greatest enemies of us alcoholics are resentment, jealousy, envy, frustration, and fear" (Alcoholics Anonymous, 1976, p. 145). In other words, the philosophy is about learning how to "live life on life's terms."
- "We absolutely insist on enjoying life" (Alcoholics Anonymous, 1976, p. 132).

Nonetheless, he found himself confused that he was still significantly struggling emotionally with living. His confusion cleared when he realized that happiness was a by-product of living a life without demands on others or circumstances to be the way he wanted them to be. In his letter to the *AA Grapevine*, he stated that the shift he had experienced resulted in the following: "Nowdays my brain no longer races compulsively in either elation, grandiosity, or depression. I have been given a quiet place in bright sunshine" (Wilson, 1958, p. 2).

BOX 2C: TWELVE STEPS OF ALCOHOLICS ANONYMOUS

1. We admitted we were powerless over alcohol—that our lives had become unmanageable.
2. Came to believe that a Power greater than ourselves could restore us to sanity.
3. Made a decision to turn our will and our lives over to the care of God as we understood Him.
4. Made a searching and fearless moral inventory of ourselves.
5. Admitted to God, to ourselves, and to another human being the exact nature of our wrongs.
6. Were entirely ready to have God remove all these defects of character.
7. Humbly asked Him to remove our shortcomings.
8. Made a list of all persons we had harmed, and became willing to make amends to them all.
9. Made direct amends to such people wherever possible, except when to do so would injure them or others.
10. Continued to take personal inventory and when we were wrong promptly admitted it.
11. Sought through prayer and meditation to improve our conscious contact with God as we understood Him, praying only for knowledge of His will for us and the power to carry that out.
12. Having had a spiritual awakening as the result of these Steps, we tried to carry this message to alcoholics, and to practice these principles in all our affairs.

Alcoholics Anonymous, Selection from "How It Works," *Alcoholics Anonymous: The Story of How Many Thousands of Men and Women Have Recovered from Alcoholism*, pp. 71-72, Alcoholics Anonymous World Services, Inc., 1939.

Some of the concepts introduced in Wilson's (1958) letter about emotional sobriety are reflected in colloquial addictionary phrases. A few examples are as follows:

- Demanding others or circumstance be the way he wanted them to be is embodied in the addictionary phrase of "taking someone's inventory." That means focusing on what someone else struggles with in living rather than focusing on one's own issues. It is related to Steps 4 and 5 of AA. An example of this is responding to discrimination experienced—"Sometimes our drinking will be used politically" (Alcoholics Anonymous, 1976, p. 145)—by looking at one's own behavior when abusing substances (Steps 4 and 5) and facing the issues of discrimination in context of a recovery community such as AA (e.g., sponsor, meetings).

- Having a "compulsively [racing brain] in either elation, grandiosity, or depression" (Wilson, 1958, p. 2) relates to the addictionary phrase of "pink clouding." This experience often occurs in the early stage of recovery (e.g., "honeymoon phase") where the person has intense feeling of happiness and euphoria at their newfound recovery. The depression (e.g., "emotional crash") occurs when they face challenges and realities that overwhelm them emotionally.

- Experiencing a balanced lifestyle that resulted in "a quiet place in the bright sunshine" (Wilson, 1958, p. 2) is reflected in the addictionary concept of "living amends," where the person lives a sober life, is no longer doing harm to others, and focuses their life on service to others both within and outside of AA. This concept is related to Steps 8 and 9 of AA.

Other Authors' Elaboration on Emotional Sobriety

Berger (2010) expands on Wilson's letter and describes clients with SUD as having a "black-and-white" life perspective as well as being perfectionists who have extremely high expectations of themselves and others. Everyone is expected to succumb to their will and desires, described as "King/Baby" (Tiebout, 1999).

This perspective may be a result of relationship trauma experienced by the client with SUD. Love both hurts and heals people in terms of their heart, mind, and spirit: "We're literally wired to experience *love*, warmth, and a sense of well-being through closeness and to *fear* abandonment." (Dayton, 2007, p. xix). Deficits in attachments and wounds of trauma impact the creation and maintenance of relationships (Compton & Patterson, 2023). Pain protection can result in interaction misinterpretation, difficulty trusting, rigid relationship boundaries, or overreacting/underreacting emotionally (Compton & Patterson, 2023). Relationship trauma results in intense emotional reactions that overwhelm people and prevent emotional sobriety (Dayton, 2007).

The "emotional merry-go-round" described by Wilson (1958) is as follows:

- Their response to the trauma was self-medicating through substances, resulting in an SUD.
- They struggle with emotional sobriety even in recovery, as Bill W. did.
- As a result of their trauma, they respond to the unwanted behavior of others and unwanted life situations with intense emotional imbalance.

Berger (2010) defines emotional sobriety as living in the "here and now" and being responsible for one's emotions and action choices. Box 2D contains Berger's list of 12 smart things to do to unhook emotional dependency.

BOX 2D: 12 SMART THINGS TO DO TO UNHOOK EMOTIONAL DEPENDENCY

12 Smart Things to Do to Unhook Emotional Dependency

1. Know yourself-and how to stay centered.
2. Stop allowing others to edit your reality.
3. Stop taking things personally.
4. Own your projections as an act of integrity.
5. Confront yourself for the sake of your integrity while practicing:
   a. *Self-support* (This stems from self-acceptance.),
   b. *Self-soothing* (This self-talk involves a balanced perspective of our human flaws.),
   c. *Self-compassion* (This means acceptance of our imperfection.)
   These three practices help us deepen our self-honesty.
6. Stop pressuring others to change, and instead pressure yourself to change.
7. Develop a healthy perspective toward yourself, your feelings, and your emotional themes.
8. Appreciate what is.
9. Comfort yourself when you are hurt or disappointed.
10. Use your personal compass to guide your life.
11. Embrace relationship tensions as the fuel for personal growth.
12. Recognize that the "problem" is not the real problem.

Adapted from Berger (2010)

Emotional sobriety means that the client with SUD is living with balance and maturity: Emotions, thoughts and actions are lived in balance (Dayton, 2007). As a result of having emotional sobriety, the recovering client with SUD takes the right action for their own integrity in unwanted interactions and situations that present themselves and accept responsibility for their feelings and actions. They are living with the philosophy "You don't get what you deserve in life, and you don't get what you don't deserve; you just get what you get."

In response to the impact of the emotional trauma on their client with SUD, the helping professional can assist in the development of intentional interactions that are not defensive (Compton & Patterson, 2023). Because emotional sobriety is impossible to achieve and maintain perfectly, the helping professional can assist the client with SUD in developing recovery community supports that assist them in the achievement and maintenance of emotional sobriety. For example, the recovering client with SUD who has relationship trauma due to abuse experienced at a young age can avoid substance use and intense emotional reactions in response to unwanted circumstances in intimate relationships (e.g., an unwanted divorce). This can be accomplished in a trusting relationship with a helping professional and SUD recovery communities.

SUD Recovery Communities

In Chapter 1, there was discussion of the important role of the helping professional in:

- assisting the client with SUD client establish recovery communities (e.g., group counseling, self-help groups)
- determining the unique amount of social interventions (of the BioPsychoSocial model) needed by the client with SUD in terms of recovery communities

This section will provide a brief overview of the establishment of the recovery community of group counseling as well as the importance of social interventions in this context. A more extensive overview of the establishment and social interventions with regard to the 12-step self-help group of Alcoholics Anonymous follows.

Group Counseling

In Chapter 1, the importance of the creation of a group counseling recovery community for the client with SUD was presented. The group counseling benefits for the client with SUD are:

- sharing similar SUD struggles with other members;
- feeling the counselor's and group members' compassion for their life story that led to the SUD and their current struggles with their SUD;
- experiencing being held accountable for their behaviors (e.g., confronted in a caring, honest, direct manner);
- learning about themselves and how they interact with others;
- experiencing confrontation directly through feedback and indirectly through other members' stories as they want the other members address their issues in group; and
- having the opportunity to drop the image they present to the world because they can't "con a con" (other group members).

This recovery community of compassionate accountability provides an opportunity for the client with SUD to have healthy interpersonal relationships instead of the unhealthy relationships they had during their active SUD experiences. The healthy relationships are genuine, real, and honest rather than manipulative and self-serving.

Group counseling is a re-creation of their family-of-origin issues and a microcosm of the real world (Yalom, 1985). That means that in group counseling the client with SUD will frequently have:

- family issues arise (e.g., female counselor confrontation of the client with SUD raises their previous struggles with an abusive alcoholic mother); and
- interpersonal issues they have with others outside the group reoccurring in group counseling because they are interacting with others in the group (e.g., another group member acts like a coworker the client with SUD dislikes).

Because the issues occur during group counseling, the interactions are observed by the group leader and other members who can give the client with SUD immediate feedback on how they are acting in this relationship. The reason the client with SUD needs group counseling in contrast with only receiving individual, couples, or family counseling is because of the unique components group counseling provides the client with SUD:

- being with other clients with SUD who are also used to manip-
  ulating people in order to have their own selfish needs met;
- having these manipulation strategies openly witnessed and
  immediately confronted; and
- experiencing the care of others who are concurrently holding
  them accountable for their behaviors.

In the caring atmosphere of group counseling, the leader and the
group members invite the client with SUD to drop their façade and
be honest, open, and genuine with them—to be who they really are.

Clients with SUD are frequently referred to group counseling
because it is a counseling format frequently used in SUD treatment
centers due to its long history in the SUD field, the benefits of it as
stated previously, and its cost effectiveness (Miller, 2021). However,
group counselors have not necessarily received specific training needed
to lead groups (e.g., group development stages and group counseling
techniques) or how to handle common SUD group counseling issues
(e.g., relapse, inappropriate responses to authority figures, mistrust
of others; Miller, 2021).

Helping professionals, then, need to make group counseling referrals
with an awareness of the resources available to the client with SUD.
They also need to be prepared to process the experience with the client
with SUD so the client can understand the experiences they are having
in relation to the group. Because the client with SUD may have a range
of experiences with group counseling in terms of quality, the helping
professional needs to make sure the client has a safe place with them
to honestly discuss their group counseling experience.

For example, the helping professional may recommend the client
with SUD receive counseling. The only treatment available to the
client, who has very little money, is group counseling provided by
the local mental health facility. The client with SUD does not want
to attend group counseling because of personal issues they want to
talk over in individual counseling, but they agree that they need SUD
treatment. The helping professional can make the group counseling
referral in this manner:

1. Explain the treatment limitations to the client with SUD client.
2. Help them prepare for attending the group.
3. Process the experience with them after they attend.

While this is not the ideal treatment that either the helping professional or the client with SUD had hoped for, the helping professional
can assist the client with learning how to live life on life's terms—an

approach that the client may need to rely on throughout their recovery process. It is also possible that in such an unfortunate circumstance, the helping professional helps the client with SUD develop an even stronger recovery community in terms of self-help groups that are explored in the next section.

12-Step Self-Help Group Alcoholics Anonymous (AA)

The organizational structure of AA is best described using the distinction drawn by Miller et al. (2019). The distinction of the structure is the 12-step program and the 12-step fellowship. Through both of these areas, addictionary terms/phrases are *italicized* in the text or in quotation marks in brackets following the term/phrase. Additionally, the 12 Traditions of Alcoholics Anonymous (Alcoholics Anonymous World Services, 1953) are listed in Box E.

BOX 2E: TWELVE TRADITIONS OF ALCOHOLICS ANONYMOUS

1. Our common welfare should come first; personal recovery depends upon A.A. unity.
2. For our group purpose there is but one ultimate authority — a loving God as He may express Himself in our group conscience. Our leaders are but trusted servants; they do not govern.
3. The only requirement for A.A. membership is a desire to stop drinking.
4. Each group should be autonomous except in matters affecting other groups or A.A. as a whole.
5. Each group has but one primary purpose — to carry its message to the alcoholic who still suffers.
6. An A.A. group ought never endorse, finance, or lend the A.A. name to any related facility or outside enterprise, lest problems of money, property, and prestige divert us from our primary purpose.
7. Every A.A. group ought to be fully self-supporting, declining outside contributions.
8. Alcoholics Anonymous should remain forever non-professional, but our service centers may employ special workers.
9. A.A., as such, ought never be organized; but we may create service boards or committees directly responsible to those they serve.

10. Alcoholics Anonymous has no opinion on outside issues; hence the A.A. name ought never be drawn into public controversy.

11. Our public relations policy is based on attraction rather than promotion; we need always maintain personal anonymity at the level of press, radio, and films.

12. Anonymity is the spiritual foundation of all our traditions, ever reminding us to place principles before personalities.

Alcoholics Anonymous World Services, *Twelve Steps and Twelve Traditions*, pp. 9-13. Copyright © 1981 by Alcoholics Anonymous World Services, Inc. Reprinted with permission.

These guidelines are intended to preserve the health of the AA group and some of them (Traditions 1, 3, 5, 7, & 12) are commented on in the text. Also, these guidelines facilitate the development of the formal fellowship present in the meetings so members have the experience of being welcomed and encouraged to have hope for their substance abuse recovery.

12-STEP PROGRAM

Bill W. (1958) writes about "working the steps" of AA. In *addictionary* terminology, this means that the SUD client is applying the steps to their lives. In a narrative form, the *Twelve Steps and Twelve Traditions* (1953) ["12 & 12"]. summarizes how the AA member works the steps of the program as highlighted in Box F.

BOX 2F: EXCERPT FROM *TWELVE STEPS AND TWELVE TRADITIONS* (ALCOHOLICS ANONYMOUS, 1953)

(Note: emphasis added by author.)

Step One showed us an amazing paradox: We found that we were totally unable to be rid of the alcohol obsession until we first admitted that we were powerless over it. In *Step Two* we saw that since we could not restore ourselves to sanity, some Higher Power must necessarily do so if we were to survive. Consequently, in *Step Three* we turned our will and our lives over to the care of God as we understood Him. For the time being, we who were atheist or agnostic discovered that our own group, or A.A. as a whole, would suffice as a higher power. Beginning with *Step Four*, we commenced to search out the things in ourselves which had brought us to physical, moral, and spiritual bankruptcy. We made a searching and fearless moral inventory. Looking at *Step Five*, we decided that an inventory, taken alone, wouldn't be enough. We knew we would have to quit the deadly business of living alone with our conflicts, and in honesty confide these to God and another human being. At *Step Six*, many of us balked—for the practical reason that we did not wish to have all our defects of character removed, because we still loved some of them too much. Yet we knew we had to make a settlement with the fundamental principle of Step Six. So we decided that while we still had some flaws of character that we could not yet relinquish, we ought nevertheless to quit our stubborn, rebellious hanging on to them. We said to ourselves, "This I cannot do today, perhaps, but I can stop crying out 'No, never!'" Then, in *Step Seven*, we humbly asked God to remove our shortcomings such as He could or would under the conditions of the day we asked. In *Step Eight*, we continued our house-cleaning, for we saw that we were not only in conflict with ourselves, but also with people and situations in the world in which we lived. We had to begin to make our peace, and so we listed the people we had harmed and became willing to set things right. We followed this up in *Step Nine* by making direct amends to those concerned, except when it would injure them or other people. By this time, at *Step Ten*, we had begun to get a basis for daily living, and we keenly realized that we would need to continue taking personal inventory, and that when we were in the wrong we ought to admit it promptly. In *Step Eleven* we saw that if a Higher Power had restored us to sanity and had enabled us to live with some peace of mind in a sorely troubled world, then such a Higher Power was worth knowing better, by as direct contact as possible. The persistent use of meditation and prayer, we found, did open the channel so that where there had been a trickle, there now was a river which led to sure power and safe guidance from God as we were increasingly better able to understand Him [*Step Twelve*].

So, practicing these Steps, we had a spiritual awakening about which finally there was no question. Looking at those who were only beginning and still doubted themselves, the rest of us were able to see the change setting in. From great numbers of such experiences, we could predict that the doubter who still claimed that he hadn't got the "spiritual angle," and who still considered his well-loved A.A. group the higher power, would presently love God and call Him by name.

Now, what about the rest of the Twelfth Step? The wonderful energy it releases and the eager action by which it carries our message to the next suffering alcoholic and which finally translates the Twelve Steps into action upon all our affairs is the payoff, the magnificent reality, of Alcoholics Anonymous.

Members of Alcoholics Anonymous describe many different ways of "working" the 12 Steps. This description, found in the book *Twelve Steps and Twelve Traditions* is just one. Others can be found on aa.org and on aagrapevine.org. Alcoholics Anonymous World Services, Excerpt from "Step Twelve," *Twelve Steps and Twelve Traditions*, pp. 107-109. Copyright © 1981 by Alcoholics Anonymous World Services, Inc. Reprinted with permission.

If the AA member works the steps, they can receive the 12 Promises (numbers added to the text by the author) that are preceded by this sentence: "As God's people we stand on our feet, we don't crawl before anyone" (AA, 1976, p. 83).

[1] If we are painstaking about this phase of our development, we will be amazed before we are half way through. [2] We are going to know a new freedom and a new happiness. [3] We will not regret the past nor wish to shut the door on it. [4] We will comprehend the word serenity and we will know peace. [5] No matter how far down the scale we have gone, we will see how our experience can benefit others. [6] That feeling of uselessness and self-pity will disappear. [7] We will lose interest in selfish things and gain interest in our fellows. [8] Self-seeking will slip away. [9] Our whole attitude and outlook upon life will change. [10] Fear of people and of economic insecurity will leave us. [11] We will intuitively know how to handle situations which used to baffle us. [12] We will suddenly realize that God is doing for us what we could not do for ourselves.

Are these extravagant promises? We think not. They are being fulfilled among us—sometimes quickly, sometimes slowly. They will always materialize if we work for them. (AA, 1976, pp. 83–84)

One way members learn how to apply the steps to their lives is by attending 12-step meetings. In all of these meetings, medallions ("chips") can be given out to acknowledge the length of time the member has in recovery ("clean time"). The time markers vary depending on factors such as the location of the group in the United States. For example, a group may give out a beginner medallion, a white poker chip, to acknowledge a "commitment to a new way of life" and other poker chips of designated colors to note 30 days, 60 days, 90 days, months, and then 1-year intervals with coin medallions to note following significant intervals, such as 1 year, 18 months, and multiple years of recovery (Miller, 2021). This is an important way to celebrate recovery, especially if the "outside world" is not acknowledging the member's recovery time.

Miller (2021) describes six types of meetings where the steps may be discussed or specifically focused on (e.g., step meetings):

- In *open meetings*, generally one recovering person speaks to the group about their addiction and recovery story, and those without SUD can attend and listen. These meetings are for people who generally want to learn more about addiction.
- *Closed meetings* are for individuals with SUD only.
- *Discussion meetings* tend to focus on a topic discussed by those with SUD in attendance; these meetings are called *participation meetings* in California.
- In *speaker meetings*, one person with SUD speaks to the audience about their addiction and recovery story; the speaker meeting may be open or closed.
- In *step meetings*, the topic for discussion is one of the 12 steps; typically, these meetings are only for people with SUD.
- In *Big Book meetings*, a chapter from *Alcoholics Anonymous* is read and discussed.

Some examples of "side benefits" to these meetings follow. First, because the only requirement for membership is a desire to stop drinking (Tradition 3), anyone can attend the meetings. Second, depending on the type of meeting, members are able to practice social skills in various ways before, during, and after the meeting as well as improve reading skills (e.g., reading from assigned meeting readings or reading the Big Book). Third, meetings may help people with the practical realities of living (e.g., finding jobs, obtaining lawyers). A humorous example of this occurring in a group was communicated to the author by an AA member:

A person attending a meeting for the first time asked the group at the beginning of the meeting, "Does anyone know a good attorney?" Every person in the room of at least 30 members raised their hand immediately. The entire group laughed loudly at the reality that each member had experienced and survived legal problems. (Anonymous, personal communication, June, 1987)

In closed meetings (ones where only alcoholics are allowed to attend), the addictionary term *home group* is used to describe the meeting the member attends regularly where other members get to know them well. As a result, home groups may enhance the side benefits listed previously because members know each other so well. The experience of a home group is described in the personal story "Women Suffer Too" in *Alcoholics Anonymous* (1976):

> I had found friends, understanding friends who often knew what I was thinking and feeling better than I knew myself, and didn't allow me to retreat into my prison of loneliness and fear over a fancied slight or hurt. Talking things over with them, great floods of enlightenment showed me myself as I really was and I was like them. (pp. 228–229)

Some addictionary terms require explaining here. *Friend of Bill W./ Friend of Bill's* is a signal letting people know that the person/activity is related to AA. For example, it may be a car bumper sticker or it may notify others in a public location (e.g., cruise ships) that there is an AA meeting at a specific time and place.

The person who leads the meeting is called the *chair*. The chair is viewed as a "trusted servant" who does not govern (Tradition 2). Typically, the chair is the individual who has volunteered for that week to coordinate the functioning of the meeting: open the meeting room, make sure the room is set up for a meeting (e.g., chairs/tables, room temperature, coffee/snacks), begin the meeting (e.g., read the opening comments to the meeting, call on members to read specific areas, such as the 12 steps), monitor the discussion (e.g., make sure the 12 Traditions are followed, no one dominates the meeting), and close the meeting (opposite activities of opening the meeting as well as activities such as collecting the money donations from members). While there are no dues or fees required, the donation consists of the member donating what they can—typically $1 per person when the collection basket is passed around during the meeting ("pass the basket"; Tradition 7).

Often in these meetings (except perhaps in open meetings), no "crosstalk" is allowed; another function of the chair is to stop this behavior. *Crosstalk* means talking directly to and/or giving unsolicited direct advice to another member during the meeting in response to what they have shared. The benefit to avoidance of crosstalk in meetings is that members learn how to "live in community" with others (Tradition 1). For example, when hearing other members' statements that they do not agree with and have emotional reactions toward, they learn how to say nothing and learn about themselves by experiencing their emotional reactions and processing them outside the meeting with other members such as sponsors ("principles before personalities"; Tradition 12).

Shares are members' experiences, challenges, and emotions related to SUD and the recovery process that are expressed in the meeting. By hearing and sharing their personal stories of struggle and success with one another, they

- gain insights both by hearing themselves talk out loud and by listening to others' recovery stories of "experience, strength, and hope";
- find and give encouragement to one another; and
- participate in community-building through honest sharing where they drop the façade of how they present themselves in the world (e.g., appearance, material possessions) and tell others how they really are, which includes asking for help to stay sober or "work the program" (e.g., let go of the past and the future and focus on living a decent lifestyle in the present).

Typically, one person shares at a time; if in a circle, one person speaks and then the person sitting next to them speaks. When a person is done sharing their comments, they often say, "Pass," which means that the next person can share, and the group typically acknowledges their share by saying, "Thank you, [name]." During this sharing time, they may hear encouraging 12-step phrases such as "Easy does it," "First things first," and "One day at a time." The phrase often directed to *newcomers*, or those who are new to the recovery program, is "Keep coming back," as evidenced in Schneker's (2009) story:

> A client of mine, a man in his early 20s with a significant addiction history, took to the 12-step program like a drowning man grabs a life preserver. Although he dutifully followed the program's precepts and the advice of

his sponsor, it was not always easy for him to give up the alluring pleasures of his former life. One day, feeling especially frustrated, he got up to speak in a meeting and spouted off. "I hate recovery! I hate AA! I hate this lifestyle! I hate everybody in this room!" As he reported it to me, he was met with a brief silence, then a chorus of "Thanks for sharing," "Keep coming back," "It works if you work it." I never expected that kind of response," he told me. "I couldn't help but crack up. Where else could I curse out a room full of people and have them be supportive of me?" (p. 217)

The member in this story gained insights by hearing himself talk out loud, found encouragement in their comments following his share, and participated in community building through the honest sharing of his struggles in recovery. The member's experience reflects a healthy AA group, as evidenced in the calm, appreciative, gentle-humored reaction to an emotionally charged share.

INFORMAL FELLOWSHIP IN 12-STEP GROUPS

We are all in the same boat on a stormy sea and we owe each other a terrible loyalty.

—*G. K. Chesterson*

In this section, the author describes the culture of AA in terms of an informal fellowship in contrast with the fellowship that occurs in the formal structure of the 12-step meeting. Again, the reader is encouraged to examine this section with a critical eye because the author is attempting to provide insider knowledge. As with any culture, it is impossible to describe the community in a simple, straightforward fashion that the helping professional reading this text can pass on readily to their client with SUD. For example, if the helping professional were to make a referral to a support group affiliated with a religious organization, while they could provide information about the religion and the organization, the actual practice of the religion and the organization would be determined by the community of support (e.g., the group).

In terms of AA, the helping professional could look at the AA website (https://aa.org) and provide accurate information about AA philosophy and organization. However, the actual 12-step group that the client with SUD attends will adapt the philosophy and the organization to their meeting. While this impacts the formal fellowship of the meeting, the "personality" of the 12-step group is also impacted by factors such as the specific culture of that group involving factors such as the group's history, membership makeup, leaders, and so on (*informal fellowship*, Tradition 4).

Throughout the referral process, the reader needs to keep focused on what helps the client with SUD stay sober and live a balanced lifestyle. Such an approach will serve as a rudder for the helping professional and the client with SUD that will assist them in navigating confusing waters as they choose together a recovery community that is the best fit for the client. It may also be reassuring to remember that no one knows all there is to know about AA culture and that each person who has knowledge of AA (e.g., professional, client with SUD, AA member) has "filtered" it through their own professional and personal experiences with the organization.

A referral to a group means that the helping professional works with the fear of the unknown experienced by the client with SUD, even if they have attended AA previously. This is necessary because in addition to each 12-step group having its own personality, the client with SUD, simply by walking into the room of the meeting, is making a public statement: "Substance use is my main life problem, and all my attempts to address it have failed." Such an admission is, at best, a humbling process that may result in the client with SUD having reactions of great shame and humiliation. That is why the fellowship, both formal and informal, is so critical to their recovery process. However, remember that because it is a self-help group, membership changes at each meeting depending on who is present, thereby impacting the fellowship experienced. With any self-help group, the helping professional can use Appendices 2C and 2D to help their client with SUD find the best match of a self-help group. Appendix 2C contains "Processing the Experience" and "Processing a Negative Experience" (Miller, 2021), while Appendix 2D contains "Guidelines for Healthy and Unhealthy Groups" (Miller, 2021).

The "more informal fellowship can be described as the pattern of interactions among members that includes sharing joys and hardships, helping out when others are in need, and enjoying social events together" (Miller et al., 2019, p. 254). This fellowship encourages sponsorship where a *sponsor*, someone who has been in the 12-step program longer and may be viewed as a mentor, can guide them through the steps (Miller, 2021). Sponsors, as well as other members of the recovery community, can help the member through difficult times where the client with SUD has an urge to use or needs to recover from a "slip" (also known as a "lapse" or "relapse") where they returned to using substances (Miller, 2021). An example of helping others in recovery (Tradition 5) is reflected in another excerpt from the "Women Suffer Too" in the Big Book: "I have something to contribute to humanity since I am peculiarly qualified, as a fellow-sufferer, to give aid and comfort to those who have stumbled and fallen over this business of meeting life" (AA, 1976, p. 229).

Self-help group sponsors/mentors, like groups, may be healthy or unhealthy. A client once stated about a 12-step group sponsor who was a poor match for them, "I'm NOT going to have someone tell me what I am to do every moment of every day I am sober." In this situation, the helping professional helped the client with SUD find a more suitable sponsor for their personality and recovery needs. The use of "Guidelines for a Healthy/Unhealthy Self-help Group Sponsor/ Mentor" in Appendix 2D (Miller, 2021) may assist in the process of finding a suitable sponsor/mentor. The helping professional needs to flexibly use these guidelines to meet the unique needs of the client with SUD.

Because anyone can be a member of AA, there is a need for the help- ing professional to encourage the client with SUD to have a protective stance similar to one they would take at any social setting where they avoid automatically trusting whoever is present. Note that this caution can be given by the helping professional to the client with SUD regard- ing any self-help group. An example of a caution is the addictionary term of "13th stepping." *13 stepping* is an intimate (taboo) romantic/ sexual relationship with another member of the 12-step group. In colloquial terms, it has meant "lying in bed after sex and talking about the other 12 steps" and typically involves preying on newcomers in recovery who are vulnerable in some way in order to obtain personal gain (e.g., sexual, financial). This behavior is considered a violation of the principles and guidelines of 12-step programs that emphasize mutual support, respect, and maintaining healthy boundaries. In healthy self-help groups, group members may intervene somehow (e.g., separate the newcomer from the member preying on them; talk with them individually) in order to preserve the safety and well-being of everyone in the group.

A summary of overall strengths and limitations of AA (based on Miller, 2021) and interventions the helping professional can use to combat limitations are listed in Table 2.1.

TABLE 2.1 Summary of AA Strengths and Limitations and Helping Professional Interventions

Potential strengths	Potential limitations	Helping professional interventions on limitations
Helps the client with SUD to interpret and apply the 12 steps to their lives.	Has rigid interpretation and application of the 12 steps to the life of the client with SUD.	-Assist them in finding another group or in finding members (e.g., sponsors) who can assist them with more flexible interpretation and application. -Find out from whom they can hear the message of a hope for SUD recovery. -Help them develop a flexible recovery program that fits their needs (e.g., avoid a rigid formula of "90 meetings in 90 days").
Has open membership and is free.	Increases the vulnerability of the clint with SUD due to unscreened and free membership.	-Process the experience of the client with SUD. -Encourage attendance of 5–6 meetings to obtain an "average" of who is present and who chairs the meeting as well as the culture of the meeting. -Encourage the development of a protective stance.
Has involved previously positive experiences for the client with SUD.	Has involved previously negative experiences for the client with SUD (e.g., has experienced discrimination).	Process previous or current negative experiences encouraging the "bigger picture" of AA beyond their group experience and/or help them find a group that fits them better.
-Is widely used (e.g., SUD treatment) and readily available to a client with SUD who finds it a good match for their SUD recovery needs (e.g., especially if White, middle class, male; comfortable with the language used both formally ["Him"/"powerlessness"] and/or informally [rule of no swearing]). -Has special interest groups (e.g., women).	Is the only support group readily available to the client with SUD who finds it a poor match for their recovery needs (e.g., especially if NOT White, middle class, male; uncomfortable with the language used both formally ["Him"/"powerlessness"] and/or informally [rule of no swearing]).	-Help them find a balance of realistic expectations of others. -Help them translate terms that are offensive to them without them feeling they are compromising their values.
Has a philosophy and guidelines for a way of living with the SUD that match well with the client with SUD (e.g., spiritual focus, Christian orientation).	Consists of a philosophy and guidelines for living with the SUD that are a mismatch with the client with SUD (e.g., spiritual focus, Christian orientation).	-Help them develop a tolerance for these group tendencies. -Help them find a group that fits them better.

The next section focuses on the impact of technology on AA. This is necessary because technological changes have had an impact on AA overall, specifically on the 12-step program in terms of meetings and fellowship, and the 12-step informal fellowship.

The Impact of Technology on Alcoholics Anonymous (AA)

For each of the areas of the 12-step program (e.g., meetings; fellowship) and the 12-step informal fellowship, positive outcomes, limitations, and health professional limitation interventions are presented. Again, the impact of technology can be examined in relation to any self-help group.

IMPACT ON 12-STEP PROGRAM

In terms of the impact of technology on meetings, it is necessary to look at AA meetings historically. Traditionally, AA meetings were, as currently named, "in-person meetings" where members developed a strong sense of community, and accountability. Some examples of these components include:

- Members participate in service activities as a part of their individual recovery program that helped the meeting function (e.g., setting up chairs, tables, etc.).
- By being physically present with one another, members (especially in a home group where members saw each other regularly) could determine how members were functioning through eye contact, touch (e.g., hugs, handshakes), and the overall "3D" experience of being in their presence.

In this version of the recovery community, shared personal connection (e.g., emotional support) and accountability of one another were both broad and deep.

AA and other self-help groups had similar experiences to those of other organizations in response to the COVID-19 pandemic. In particular, the pandemic impacted AA's long-standing pattern of in-person community development. Overnight, members were unable to meet in person with their recovery community. Often, they were told by well-intentioned professionals and laypersons, "Just go to an online meeting." These individuals were unaware of the inherent losses for a member accustomed to in-person meetings: the strong sense of community that could not be easily replaced through an online meeting.

Each member accustomed to in-person meetings prior to the pandemic had to make hard choices regarding if and how to be a member in an online recovery community. For example, some members chose to only have phone contact with other members until in-person meetings reopened. When in-person meetings were held again, members had to learn how to talk and express emotions (e.g., tears) while wearing masks. Other members, who had access to and were comfortable with the technology, attended online meetings. Eventually, meetings took different formats (e.g., in person, online, hybrid). Currently, AA members have a menu of options regarding meeting format. This increased technology use was in sharp contrast to AA's lifetime history of an in-person recovery community. Also, this increased shift to use of an online meeting format inherently impacted the formal fellowship connections made during an AA meeting. An example of the significant changes to the 12-step program of AA is that it is now possible for an AA member who has joined AA since the pandemic occurred to have never attended and never attend an in-person meeting for their entire recovery.

There are positive outcomes as well as limitations related to technology change impact on the 12-step program. Positive outcomes for online meetings include:

- enhanced accessibility and convenience of meetings due to a lack of barriers (e.g., distance/transportation issues, physical limitations/health concerns);
- increased sense of personal safety due to anonymity (e.g., disabled camera or use of the stop video button on Zoom to present a blank screen instead of a facial image); and
- broadened sense of community (e.g., international meetings that draw members from various countries).

An example of a broadened community would be if someone who was born/raised in Ireland and living as an adult in the United States recognizes the voice/face of a childhood friend in Ireland when attending an online meeting. Through attending the online meeting, they reconnect with each other after many years, discovering that both of them were recovering from alcohol use disorder. This reconnection would not have happened via an in-person meeting because neither traveled to the other's country of residence.

Limitations of online meetings include:

- extremely large meetings (e.g., over 100 members in attendance, thereby severely limiting the sharing of personal experiences)
- internet problems (e.g., connection, navigation)
- increased distractions (e.g., sounds/activities the member experiences in their physical setting while in an online meeting)

In addition, there may be concerns regarding anonymity and confidentiality; unknown repercussions on members for personal information they share during the meeting; and unknown consequences to members who have been involved in illegal drug use (Miller, 2021).

There are a number of helping professional limitation interventions available. First, the helping professional can assist clients with SUD by talking with them about their meeting needs, their experiences with different types of meetings, and the pros/cons for them in terms of the different types of meetings. For example, the helping professional may have a client with SUD who refuses to attend an in-person meeting. The helping professional can invite them to describe what they need in a meeting in order to stay sober, their history with in-person meetings, and the pros/cons of attending an in-person meeting. Finally, the helping professional may encourage the client with SUD to try attending an in-person meeting once to see what the experience is like and then process the experience with them.

IMPACT ON INFORMAL FELLOWSHIP

In the area of informal fellowship where AA members interact with one another through activities and roles described previously, there are also positive outcomes and limitations connected with the technology changes. Positive outcomes include:

- numerous electronic devices that clients with SUD use to connect with their recovery community;
- numerous websites and apps (e.g., mindfulness, daily gratitude) that assist them in their recovery;
- various communication forms (e.g., calling, emailing, texting) that expand their recovery community and enhance the immediacy of support from the recovery community;
- various social media forms (e.g., Facebook, Twitter, Instagram, TikTok) that expand their recovery community and help them

obtain psychoeducational information provided by organizations related to recovery; and

- various types of social media groups that limit the viewing of posts to other group members, thereby expanding their recovery community while offering protected sharing.

Miller (2021) reports limitations such as (a) increased interpersonal problems when the tendencies of clients with SUD (e.g., poor impulse control, emotional intensity, especially early in recovery) are paired with the speed of electronic messaging and (b) increased communication problems due to diminished eye contact, vocal expression, and physical touch that enhances the "sharp edge" of words written electronically (e.g., assumptions made, feelings hurt).

Additional limitations include (a) reduction of informal connections made before and after in-person meetings (e.g., members can rely on electronic messaging contact or immediate loss of contact at the end of online meetings) and (b) tendencies of AA members to make assumptions about other AA members based on age or length of recovery (e.g., older AA members or those who have been in long-term recovery are uncomfortable with the use of technology; younger AA members or those new to recovery are comfortable with the use of technology). Note that those AA members who are more comfortable with technology can be of service to other members by helping them make the technology transitions required to establish a recovery community, and members more comfortable with in-person dynamics can be of service to those members who are less comfortable with that arena.

There are many ways the helping professional can assist their clients with SUD in developing and enhancing their informal fellowship. Helping professional limitation interventions include:

- asking clients what electronic devices they have and their comfort in using them;
- finding out the websites and apps they are aware of, what they find helpful about them, and then providing them with information that is obtained by exploring website and applications with them or information that has been obtained from colleagues or professional organizations;
- determining the social media forms they are comfortable with and use of psychoeducational social media (e.g., additional information that can be provided to them that they find helpful and necessary to their recovery);

- finding out their social media group memberships and discussing the pros and cons of such memberships; and
- assisting clients in slowing down their reaction time to electronic messaging (e.g., starting message exchanges or responding to messages by waiting an hour and/or talking to their sponsor or another person in recovery first).

In summary, the impact of technology on AA has been significant. This impact will continue as technology develops and AA responds to the issues raised in response to the impact. The reader is encouraged to stay abreast of such changes through the organization of AA and their professional organizations as well as insider knowledge that is obtained from experienced members of AA.

SUMMARY

This chapter presented information that (a) integrated paraprofessional and professional knowledge and experience by using colloquial expressions of the SUD recovery community of AA, (b) enhanced understanding of the concept of emotional sobriety, and (c) increased the reader's knowledge base of the recovery communities of group counseling and self-help groups that help in the development of a balanced lifestyle of serenity and hope for the client with SUD.

KEY POINTS

1. The impact of the potential lens of the helping professional as they work with their SUD population was explored. Addictionary terms and phrases were used to bridge insider knowledge and experience with outsider knowledge using the colloquial expressions of the SUD recovery community of AA.
2. The overall concept of emotional sobriety as well as related concepts (e.g., relationship trauma), were defined. The impact of emotional sobriety on the recovery process of the client with SUD was discussed in order to assist the client in developing a lifestyle of balance and maturity.
3. The importance of the development of the SUD recovery communities of group counseling and self-help groups (e.g., AA) for the client with SUD was highlighted. This network of support is necessary for the client to obtain and maintain their recovery. The

helping professional has a critical role in the development of the SUD recovery community because the recovery community support network needs to fit the unique recovery needs of the client.

Be responsible for the effort, not the outcome.

—*Geri Miller*

INTERACTIVE READER COMPONENTS

Case Study 2.1

Your client with SUD has been in recovery a number of years but continues to have significant difficulties in relationships with others at both home and work. They do not understand why they struggle when they work so hard to be different from when they were active in their SUD. You want to use the concept of emotional sobriety and related concepts such as relationship trauma with your client. Use the following questions to guide you in this process:

1. How would you explain the concepts of emotional sobriety and relationship trauma to them?
2. How would you explore these concepts with them?
3. How might you use Berger's (2010) list of 12 smart things to do to unhook emotional dependency in Box 2E to assist them in their recovery?

Case Study 2.2

Make yourself this case study. Think about your main struggle in life that expresses itself in behavior that bothers you and possibly others. You are aware you need to change your behavior, but you are now being told that you need to change this behavior ASAP and that you need to plan to change it for the rest of your life. You have tried to change this behavior on your own without success. Use these questions to assist you in expanding your self-awareness:

1. How would you use the information in this chapter to help you make the changes you need to make?
2. If you decided to attend a self-help group that focused on your life struggle, what would it be like for you to enter a self-help group meeting and have the experience that just upon entering everyone knows what your main life issue is?

Exercise 2.1

Develop a sample list of drug terms and their definitions that are typically used by the SUD population with whom you intend to work or with whom you are working. You may want to brainstorm list items with helping professionals who are working with your population.

Exercise 2.2

Read the first 164 pages of the Big Book (Alcoholics Anonymous, 1976) and one personal story. Explore your reactions to the readings, and if possible, discuss them with another individual. Focus on how your reactions reflect your personal and professional views of SUD and clients with SUD. Finally, explore/discuss how these reactions may impact your referrals to the SUD recovery communities of group counseling and self-help groups.

Exercise 2.3

Attend a self-help group meeting for SUD from the list of six types of meetings (open; closed; discussion; speaker; step; Big Book). Attend both an in-person and an online meeting. Be aware of all of your experiences (and reactions to them) from the beginning of finding out a meeting location through the contact with individuals after the meeting. Discuss your reactions with another individual.

Exercise 2.4

Choose one of the websites listed in the Resources/Websites section of this chapter. Spend time exploring the website to discover how it might assist you as an SUD professional and how it might be useful to you in your work with your SUD population.

SUGGESTED READINGS

Readings (Overall)

Alcoholics Anonymous. (2001). *Alcoholics Anonymous* (4th ed.). Alcoholics Anonymous World Services.

> This main text of Alcoholics Anonymous is divided into two main sections. The first section of 164 pages has 11 chapters that

cover the theory of alcoholism, a proposed solution, focus on different populations, and pragmatic approaches to recovery. The second section consists of three groupings of personal stories. There is a preface, four forewords (one for each edition), and seven appendices.

Miller, G. (2021). *Learning the language of addiction counseling* (5th ed.). Wiley.

This book has 15 chapters and is accompanied by 16 videos (one overview video and one video for each chapter) where the author explains the purpose of the book and chapter contents in less than 10 minutes. It also has teacher resources (e.g., PowerPoint, test bank) for each chapter. Chapters of particular interest include: Chapter 3 (assessment and diagnosis); Chapter 4 (co-occurring disorders and behavioral addictions); Chapter 5 (the core treatment process of addictions); Chapter 8 (self-help groups); and Chapter 12 (incorporating spirituality into addiction counseling).

Miller, W. R., Forcehimes, A. A., & Zweben, A. (2019). *Treating addiction: A guide for professionals* (2nd ed.). Guilford.

This text has four sections addressing the treatment of addiction. Section 1 has three chapters on basic addiction-related information; Section 2 has five chapters on addiction treatment; Section 3 has 10 chapters on evidence-based treatment options; and Section 4 has seven chapters on professional issues.

Reynolds, N. (2018). *I love you—but not your addiction*. Beach Front.

There are 20 chapters in this book that describe an interpersonal approach to responding to the impact of addiction on both the individual with SUD and those who care for them. It presents information on the dynamics of addiction and specific suggestions for responding in a healthy manner to both the person with SUD and the addiction dynamics. The book contains contracts, exercises, and blogs created by the author previously for a hospital blog site.

Schenker, M. D. (2009). *A clinician's guide to 12-step recovery: Integrating 12-step programs into psychotherapy*. Norton.

In this text, there are 10 chapters that focus on various aspects of 12-step recovery that a mental health professional can incorporate readily into their clinical practice.

Readings (Emotional Sobriety)

Berger, A. (2010). *12 smart things to do when the booze and drugs are gone.* Hazelden.

> This book contains an introduction explaining emotional sobriety that is divided into 12 sections (one for each of the "smart things to do") and has a concluding chapter.

Dayton, T. (2007). *Emotional sobriety.* Health Communications.

> The first chapter defines emotional sobriety, and the next 22 chapters cover a variety of topics related to the framework of emotional sobriety presented.

Readings (Recovery Story)

Moyers, W. C., & Ketcham, K. (2006). *Broken: My Story of Addiction and Redemption.* Viking.

> This book is an autobiography of the author's addiction and recovery. He is the son of journalist Bill Moyers. There is a section in the book where the author reports the sharp contrast in others' reactions to his diagnoses of SUD and cancer.

Readings (Substance Use Impact on the Brain)

Hart, C. H., & Ksir, C. J. (2018). *Drugs, society, & human behavior* (18th ed.). McGraw Hill.

> This book consists of 18 chapters. One section in particular ("How Drugs Work") has two relevant chapters: "The Nervous System" and "The Actions of Drugs."

RESOURCES/WEBSITES

Abstinence-Based 12-Step Groups

Alcoholics Anonymous (AA)

> https://aa.org

Alcoholics Anonymous (AA)—"International Guide"

> https://aa.org/aa-around-the-world

Cocaine Anonymous (CA)

https://www.ca.org

Crystal Meth Anonymous (CMA)

https://www.norcalcma.org

Heroin Anonymous (HA)

https://heroinanonymous.org/contact/

Marijuana Anonymous (MA)

https://marijuana-anonymous.org

Narcotics Anonymous (NA)

https://na.org

Spiritually Specific Abstinence-Based Self-Help Groups

Alcoholics Victorious (Christian-centered 12-step recovery program)

https://alcoholicsvictorious.org

Calix Society (Christian-centered [Catholic] 12-step recovery program)

https://calixsociety.org

Celebrate Recovery (Christian-centered 12-step recovery program)

https://celebraterecovery.com

Overcomers Outreach (Christian-centered 12-step recovery program)

https://overcomersoutreach.org

Red Road Recovery (Christian-centered Native recovery program)

https://theredroad.org

Refuge Recovery (a recovery program based in Buddhist principles/ practices)

https://refugerecovery.org

12-Step Alternative Groups
Secular Organizations for Sobriety (SOS)

https://sossobriety.org

16 Steps

https://charlottekasl.com

Self-Management and Recovery Training (SMART Recovery)

https://smartrecovery.org

Women for Sobriety (WFS)/Men for Sobriety (MFS)

https://womenforsobriety.org
https://2994002.site123.me

Harm Reduction Group
Medication Assisted Recovery Anonymous (MARA)

https://mara-international.org

12-Step Support Groups
Adult Children of Alcoholics World Service Organization (ACA)

https://adultchildren.org

Al-Anon Family Group Headquarters (Al-Anon)

https://al-anon.org

Co-Dependents Anonymous (CODA)

https://coda.org

Families Anonymous

https://familiesanonymous.org

Nar-Anon Family Group Headquarters (Nar-Anon)

https://nar-anon.org

Appendices

The lists in Appendices 2A and 2B were developed in 2023 by Miller, G.; Kent, A., Melino, R., & Reagan, A.

Appendix 2A: Drug Terms

SUBSTANCES ABUSED

Benzodiazepines: These are prescription drugs used for anxiety and sedation. *Bars/ladders* is a slang term for benzodiazepines, usually Xanax, because they resemble ladders, as they are skinny with horizontal lines resembling rungs. *Footballs* is a slang term that is used to describe small, round, blue Xanax pills. *School bus* is a slang term used to describe extra strength Xanax bars that are yellow in color; colloquially speaking, these are sometimes described as "industrial strength."

Methamphetamine: *Chalk and crank* are slang terms for this stimulant drug.

Cocaine: *Nose candy* and *blow* are slang terms for this stimulant drug. *Bricks* is a slang term that describes large quantities of cocaine. *Crack* is a highly addictive form of cocaine, usually smoked, which produces an intense but short-lived high.

Dope: This is a slang term for illegal drugs, typically referring to substances like cocaine, heroin, methamphetamine, or marijuana.

Fentanyl: This is a synthetic opioid pain medication prescribed for severe pain management. Illicitly manufactured fentanyl is a potent and dangerous drug responsible for a significant number of opioid-related overdoses. Its high potency requires extreme caution during detoxification and treatment. *China girl* is a slang term for Fentanyl.

Ganja: This is a slang term for marijuana that is derived from the Hindi word *gānjhā*.

Goofballs: This slang term for a combination of drugs typically refers to a mixture of barbiturates and amphetamines.

Mary Jane: This is a slang term for marijuana/cannabis.

Moke: This slang term describes the mix of cannabis and tobacco.

Opioids: Opioids produce pain relief and feelings of euphoria. They can be prescription pain medications or illegal drugs like heroin. *Smack* is a slang term for black tar heroin. *Sizzurp* and *lean* are slang terms for codeine cough syrup.

Psychedelics: This category of drugs consists of a number of hallucinogens. *Rainbows* is a slang term for psychedelic drugs, particularly referring to hallucinogens like LSD. *Purple haze* is a slang term for LSD. *Molly* is a slang term for MDMA.

Sauce: This is a slang term for alcohol.

Speedball: This slang term refers to heroin mixed with cocaine.

Appendix 2B: Drug-Related Terms

DRUG-RELATED TERMS: PEOPLE AND LOCATION

People
Dealer/pusher: a person who illicitly sells drugs to others. *Dopeman* is a colloquial term for a drug dealer, and *snowman* is a colloquial term for a cocaine drug dealer.

Geeker: a person who regularly uses stimulant drugs and exhibits hyperactive or nervous behavior.

Space cadet: a person who uses increased amounts of benzodiazepines.

Snow bunny: someone who abuses cocaine or other white powdery drugs.

Zombie: a person who uses drugs heavily and appears lethargic, disconnected, and unresponsive due to the influence of drugs; it may be especially used to describe someone on depressants.

Location
Dope house: a location where drugs are sold, distributed, or used.

DRUG-RELATED TERMS: PROCESS AND IMPACT

Process

Cooking: This is the process of preparing and manufacturing illicit drugs (such as methamphetamine, crack cocaine) that involves chemical reactions or heating substances to create a new substance. It also refers to the preparation of heroin, usually in a spoon, to make the drug injectable. Finally, certain pills also must be "cooked" in order turn them from a solid into a liquid that can be injected.

Rig: This process involves preparing and using a hypodermic needle to inject drugs.

Impact

Cold turkey: to quit or withdraw from drug use abruptly and without any gradual reduction or support.

Having the shakes: having physical symptoms associated with drug withdrawal, characterized by trembling hands or other body parts.

K-hole: a phrase used to describe the dissociative high experienced while on a high dose ketamine.

Tripping: feeling the effects of psychedelics.

Rolling: being high on the psychedelic MDMA.

Suicide Sunday: A phrase used to describe the after effects or withdrawals from using MDMA.

Strung out: being high on drugs.

Tweaker/tweeking: Description of someone under the influence of stimulant drugs, like methamphetamine, who displays restless and erratic behavior.

Appendix 2C: Questions for Processing Self-Help Group Experiences

PROCESSING THE GROUP EXPERIENCE

The following questions are adapted from Miller (2021, p. 254).

Questions to ask the client with SUD to process the group experience:

- What was the meeting like overall (e.g., friendly, hospitable)?
- What was the meeting like physically (e.g., safe part of town, easy parking, comfortable room, too much smoke in the room)?*
- How were you greeted (e.g., respectfully, friendly manner)?
- Was there anyone in the group with whom you felt particularly comfortable (i.e., potential sponsor/mentor)?
- What was the topic of the meeting (i.e., relevance to recovery)?
- Did everyone participate in the meeting (i.e., everyone spoke)?
- Did you feel comfortable with the person (people) who seemed to officially or unofficially direct the meeting (i.e., reasonable leader)?
- Did you go early and/or stay late at the meeting (i.e., have informal visits with others)?
- What were the unwritten rules of the group (i.e., swearing, introduction terms used, openness to discuss all drugs used, etc.)? Were these comfortable rules for you?

*Applies to in-person meetings only.

PROCESSING A NEGATIVE EXPERIENCE

The following questions are adapted from Miller (2021, p. 255).

Questions to ask the client with SUD who has had a negative group experience:

- What upset you about the meeting?
- Who upset you at the meeting?
- Did the incident occur before, during, or after the meeting?
- What negative feelings (shame, guilt, sadness, etc.) arose for you? How did/are you handling those feelings?
- Do you plan to return to the meeting? If so, how do you plan to address the issue? If you do not plan to return, where will you go for recovery support?

- Do you have concerns about the incident being discussed in the "self-help grapevine" (i.e., the tendency of self-help group members to talk with others in recovery about what happened in a meeting)?

Appendix 2D: Guidelines for Healthy and Unhealthy Groups and Sponsor/Mentor

GUIDELINES FOR HEALTHY AND UNHEALTHY GROUPS
The following guidelines are adapted from Miller (2021, p. 256).

Indicators of an Unhealthy Group:

- an unwelcoming sense to the group
- no greetings for newcomers or greetings that seem manipulative in nature
- an unhappy, negative tone to the majority of the group members
- an unwillingness by group members to discuss practical, optimistic approaches to recovery issues
- dominance by one or a few individuals who do not encourage participation by others
- a general lack of participation and/or interest in the meeting

Indicators of a Healthy Group:

- a welcoming to the group that makes the member feel needed and wanted, safe, and cared for
- genuine greetings of welcome by the group
- presence of a "spirit of recovery" tone that invites hope, consisting of a recovery focus and a commitment to enjoying sobriety
- a practical, optimistic approach to recovery issues by group members
- encouragement of participation of all group members who want to participate and careful listening of members' shares
- enthusiasm of members about the meeting and willingness to be supportive to one another

GUIDELINES FOR A HEALTHY/UNHEALTHY GROUP SPONSOR/MENTOR

The following guidelines are adapted from Miller (2021, p. 258).

An Unhealthy Sponsor/Mentor:

- promises *always* to be available for the person
- views sponsorship as a legitimate means to control another person
- uses sponsorship as a means to use a person in recovery (i.e., for sexual or financial gratification)
- discourages the person to think for [themself]; rather, the individual tells the person what to think and how to act
- has unrealistic expectations of a person's recovery
- is unavailable to the person
- is highly critical and judgmental of the person
- has a relatively short recovery time (less than a year sober)

A Healthy Sponsor/Mentor:

- is realistic about expectations of oneself and the sponsee
- views sponsorship as a role modeling of recovery
- sets firm, clear boundaries that prevent either one from using the other
- explores problem-solving options (rather than simplistic ones) with the sponsee
- is available, supportive, and has significant recovery time from which to draw on their recovery experiences

THE USE OF STORY/
METAPHOR, HUMOR,
EXPERIENTIAL ACTIVITY/
PLAY, AND MUSIC

OBJECTIVES

1. Using a self-care framework of the four-legged stool with clients with SUD to develop a balanced lifestyle in recovery that broadens their perspective and deepens the meaning of their lives.
2. Understanding guidelines for the use of the creative techniques to invite healing in clients with SUD and avoid harming them.
3. Learning specific creative techniques in the four areas of story and metaphor; humor; experiential activity and play; and music.

The point is, art never stopped a war and never got anybody a job. That was never its function. Art cannot change events. But it can change people. It can affect people so that they are changed ... because people are changed by art—enriched, enabled, encouraged—they then act in a way that may affect the course of events ... by the way they vote, they behave, the way they think.

—*Leonard Bernstein, John Gruen interview in the* Los Angeles Times, *December 31, 1972*

Overview of the Chapter

As discussed in Chapter 1, clients/patients with SUD use substances to feel good as well as to feel less bad (Schumacher & Williams, 2020). Chapter 2 highlights the importance of hope for the person with SUD in recovery as expressed in the 12-step program fellowship (Schenker, 2009) and the second step of the 12-step program where belief in a Higher Power implies hope for the person with SUD. Also noted in both Chapters 1 and 2 is that their recovery requires activities that expand their perspective beyond the use of substances—activities that bring them hope and joy.

The concepts of self-care, creativity, and creative techniques explored in this chapter overlap in numerous ways, making distinct boundaries between them impossible. The concept of flow will be used as a bridge of integration among these three areas: self-care, creativity, and creative techniques.

In a review of the literature, Miller (2021) discusses the impact of flow on creativity. *Flow* involves "skills, concentration, and perseverance—an activity where one can become lost" (Csikszentmihalyi, 1999, p. 825). Both novelty and accomplishment are present when one is experiencing flow. Flow increases "skill development, overall wellness, life satisfaction, emotional regulation, motivation and intrinsic motivation and [results in] decreases in anxiety and depression" (Craigen, 2023, p. 47). Craigen (2023) defines *psychological flow* as "being in the zone" where perception of time changes (moves faster or more slowly) and provides one with a sense of control over their environment. Flow also helps us witness our negative thoughts and connect with our creativity (Miller, 2021).

> The key question isn't "What fosters creativity?" But it is "Why in God's name isn't everyone creative?" Where was the human potential lost? How was it crippled? I think therefore a good question might be not why do people create, but why do people not create or innovate? We have got to abandon that sense of amazement in the face of creativity, as if it were a miracle if anybody created anything. (Maslow, 1998, p. 13)

There is evidence at the global level that the arts improve health and well-being by preventing ill health; promoting health; and helping manage and treat stress throughout one's life (Fancourt & Finn, 2019). Dayton (2007) summarizes creativity as:

- helping us envision what we want in life and steps we can take toward that dream
- allowing our knowledge to be connected to novel approaches
- using divergent thinking (e.g., being detached, changing the method of previous problem solving) that results in different paths of reasoning/imaging
- occurring when our thinking is "toned down" (e.g., sleeping)

Health professionals can use the creative arts (e.g., experiential activities) to provide educational SUD information in an enjoyable manner to individuals. These approaches have been found to positively impact views of change efforts, substance abuse, and people with SUD (Bell et al., 2014; Warren et al., 2012). Health professionals can also encourage creativity in an SUD population that may consist of novelty seekers (Dayton, 2007). The creative arts can be used to intervene (Leung et al., 2018); enhance recovery commitment, changed lifestyle, and hope (Stuebing et al., 2020); prevent relapse (Tam et al., 2016); and enhance engagement, treatment outcome, and internal motivation to change (Hawk, 2022).

Although distinct boundaries cannot be made between the concepts of self-care, creativity, and creative techniques, they are separated into sections here in order to make it less confusing to the reader.

This chapter opens with the self-care framework of the four-legged stool because of the importance of people with SUD learning balance in their recovery through self-care. One of the legs of the stool is that of the mind, emotions, and spirit. It is this leg that is impacted by the creative techniques used by the helping professional with the person with SUD. Creative techniques can both heal and harm because they circumvent the defense structures that the person with SUD uses to protect themselves; that is why they need to be used with care and respect of the powerful mediums they are. Because of their power to deeply heal as well as harm, specific guidelines are suggested for the helping professional to use that encourage healing and reduce the chances of harm. These guidelines are then followed by an exploration of the four creative techniques chosen: story and metaphor; humor; experiential activity and play; and music. Each of the techniques can provide them with hope that motivates them to change (Miller et al., 2019).

Each of these forms of creative techniques helps people be present in the moment of the experience and remember what they are learning about themselves. In Box 3A, Craigen (2023) recommends specific techniques.

> ## BOX 3A: CRAIGEN'S (2023) RECOMMENDED TECHNIQUES
>
> - Include activities of focus/concentration (mindfulness, meditation).
> - Brainstorm activities that encourage flow (challenging but within their skill level).
> - Encourage activities that provide immediate feedback (active ones such as drawing or running).
> - Provide time in session for such activities (e.g., drawing, writing) and reflecting on them.

Helping professionals aware of the power of these four creative techniques (story and metaphor; humor; experiential activity and play; and music) and their impact on clients/patients with SUD can use them with respect for the powerful, idiosyncratic experiences they can stimulate in each client. For example, music that has lyrics (whether they are sung in the song or simply "heard" because the tune and lyrics are very familiar) may have a different impact on our clients/patients individually. Therefore, we need to closely observe their verbal and nonverbal reactions in order to determine how the technique is impacting them. We also need to make sure that they have time to process their reactions, stopping the session if there is a powerful reaction to the technique and providing them with time to process the experience.

Three suggestions for you, the reader, to consider as you read this chapter are:

- Recount how you experience flow in your life and encourage it with your SUD population.
- Consider how you allow the expression of creativity in your life as well as how you encourage your SUD population to express it.
- Examine your personal use of creative techniques (story and metaphor; humor; experiential activity and play; and music) and the inclusion of these techniques in your work with your SUD population.

The stress management tip in Box 3B encourages the use of these creative techniques for the health professional.

BOX 3B: STRESS MANAGEMENT TIP

In your self-examination of the use of creative techniques in your daily life, reflect on:

1. What story of my life do I tell others at work? At home? In other social interactions?
2. How do I express **humor** at work? At home? In other social interactions?
3. What activities are enjoyable (**fun**) for me at work? At home? In other social interactions?
4. How do I include **music** at work? At home? In other social interactions?
5. What barriers are there to my creativity? How can I work around them?

Author Personal Reflections

This was a difficult chapter to write because I needed to make choices regarding creative techniques that can be used with the client with SUD. The three most difficult aspects were (a) deciding what areas to include; (b) determining guidelines for their use that ensure the well-being of the client; and (c) experiencing concern that the reader will view such techniques as unnecessary and time-consuming due to personal biases and/or professional contexts that undermine humanistic principals and encourage the values of efficiency and money.

I decided to include areas that I experienced both in the classroom as a teacher/workshop presenter with my students/participants as well as in the clinical setting that assisted my clients in learning and remembering concepts: story/metaphor; humor; experiential activity/play; and music. For example, years ago I conducted a week-long training with SUD professionals. Years after the training, I crossed paths professionally with one of the participants at the training. The person said, "I learned a LOT from you in the training, but what I remember most is the story that you told us at the end of the training." I had expected the person to remember more of the actual content of the training, but they remembered the story that captured the content. It was the story that had withstood the test of time. It was then that I began to realize the power of creative techniques.

I have also been amazed that adults are not encouraged to play/ participate in an activity just for fun and enjoyment. It was during my 32 years as a university professor teaching counseling skills to graduate students that I began to invite my students in my 3-hour classes to spend their 15-minute break taking part in some type of fun, playful exercise with me. I brought numerous toys (e.g., Hula-Hoops, Frisbees, footballs, bubbles) and games (e.g., ping-pong) to the classroom from which they could choose (or not) to use on the break. One day, a blind student told me during a break of their long-standing desire and interest in learning to use a Hula-Hoop. We spent the break using the Hula-Hoop together because he learned to use it in less than 5 minutes. He later told me, "I learned that you must push yourself and that you don't know that you *can* do something until you try." This experience taught me about the power of play, which enhanced their sense of empowerment ("I did it!") and social connection (e.g., they began to use the Hula-Hoop with other students on the break).

The guidelines for the use of these techniques result from literature reviews as well as clinical experiences of mine and others. Over time, I became aware of how clients were harmed by the well-intentioned creative techniques of professionals. I began to encourage others to make sure their clients were safe no matter what. This was anchored in the feedback given to me by one of my mentors years ago who told me during one of our supervision meetings, "I do NOT care how brilliantly you use techniques in your sessions. I care that your clients can safely reenter the world after a session with you." That feedback, stated earlier in this book, encouraged me to make sure I followed guidelines for the use of creative techniques that facilitated healing and reduced the chances of harm.

Finally, with regard to my concern of these techniques as unnecessary and time-consuming, I simply hope that the reader keeps an open mind to techniques that may be a "stretch" for them simply because it is that specific approach that may reach a client. This can also lay a foundation of lifelong learning and training skill development in these various creative techniques. As stated in the opening quote of this chapter, such experiences, I believe, assist the client in changing because creativity is a bridge—a bridge of humanness where we refuse to let them "worry alone" and instead invite them to participate in a creative experience with us. Through these experiences, the client is enriched, enabled, and encouraged to think differently and act in ways that shift their way of being in the world and experiencing the world. I have experienced such changes in myself as a client and have watched such changes occur in my clients. My hope is that you, the reader, can be wonderfully "contagious" with your clients in terms of hope for living as you use such creative approaches in your work that may last a lifetime for your clients by changing them forever.

I also made a change in the format of this chapter from the previous two chapters. In this chapter, each section of the creative techniques begins with a quote and a condensed story of a famous individual interviewed for the book *The Harder They Fall* (Stromberg & Merrill, 2005). The four individuals chosen were paired with one of the four technique sections according to their profession (e.g., a famous musician was paired with the music technique section). Their stories were selected because they were comfortable with their personal stories of their SUD struggles and recovery being shared publicly. Note that early editions of *Alcoholics Anonymous* have a story about a sculptor ("A New Vision for Sculptor") and a musician ("Smile with Me, at Me").

In conclusion, the music section is explored more extensively in terms of resources and references in order to provide the reader with an example of what the reader can do independently with regard to the other three areas of story and metaphor, humor, and experiential activity and play. This limit respects the focus of this book and the specialty areas of story and metaphor, humor, and experiential activity and play.

Self-Care Framework of the Four-Legged Stool

Typically, people with an active SUD do not practice healthy self-care in terms of their bodies because they are focused on the substance. In recovery they need to develop a realistic, flexible self-care practice that involves an ongoing commitment to making incremental changes to the development of a healthy lifestyle. Self-care can be viewed from the perspective of a four-legged stool (Miller, 2023; see Figure 3.1).

This stool has three legs that are related to body self-care (diet, exercise, sleep; Weir, 2017) and one leg that contains the mind, emotions, and spirit. All four legs facilitate resilience in the person with SUD. Miller (2021) makes specific suggestions for the body self-care (diet, exercise, sleep). The fourth leg enhances resilience because of the incorporation of "the *mind* (e.g., life-enhancing activities), *emotions* (e.g., support networks), and the *spirit* (e.g., positive activities and people

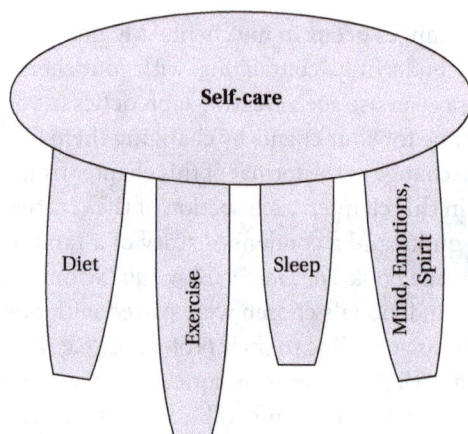

FIGURE 3.1. Self-Care

who make one feel alive, interested in living, and willing to face the day)" (Miller, 2023, p. 104).

Health professionals can use the four-legged stool as a means to teach the person with SUD about healthy self-care. It can be used in many ways, including as an educational tool, for session check-in, and the maintenance of a balanced recovery lifestyle. Box 3C contains an example of its use.

BOX 3C: FOUR-LEGGED STOOL QUESTIONS ENCOURAGING SELF-CARE REFLECTION (MILLER, 2023)

In terms of diet, exercise, sleep, and overall resilience (e.g., care of mind, emotions, and spirit):

1. What routines/rituals are helpful to you?
2. What is the best way to start your day?
3. How might you regain your balance during the day if you lose it?
4. When you are afraid, ask yourself these safety questions:
   o Who feels safe to me right now?
   o Where is a safe place for me right now?
5. What sensory experiences can you use to calm yourself (e.g., sight, hearing, taste, touch, smell)?

Guidelines for the Use of Creative Techniques

The "North Star Guide" (i.e., based on the five principles of the APA's ethics code; McNally & Cochrane, 2023) may assist the reader in developing guidelines for the use of creative techniques with their SUD population. The five principles of the APA's ethics code (APA, 2017) are listed below in a condensed format where two of them have informal phrases in parens (McNally & Chochrane, 2023):

- Principle A: beneficence/nonmaleficence ("Do good, don't do bad.")
- Principle B: trust ("Be responsible for your actions.")
- Principle C: integrity
- Principle D: justice
- Principle E: respect for people's rights and dignity

The APA Code of Ethics can be accessed at https://www.apa.org/ethics/code/

McNally and Cochrane (2023) state that practicing ethically does NOT mean practicing perfectly, but it does mean practicing reasonably.

As we employ creative techniques in our practice, we need to be aware of three types of cognitive biases that may impact us (McNally & Cochrane, 2023):

- **Availability:** This is where we assume information about the person with SUD and "find what we look for." This involves *confirmation bias,* where we seek evidence to confirm our hypothesis. For example, as we employ the technique of humor, because we find a joke funny and we have told it to other people with SUD who have found it funny, we assume the person with SUD hearing it will also find it funny.
- **Anchoring:** This is where we are overly dependent on our first impressions and allow the first perspective we hear about a person with SUD or what we see when we look at them influence the approach we take. An example here is seeing a person with SUD who is disheveled and angry and assuming the use of the technique of storytelling will not appeal to them.
- **Representativeness:** This is where information is emphasized that fits our idea of what is typical. Here we could assume that because the person with SUD is experiencing a terrible loss in their life, they have no interest in participating in the technique of play.

Awareness of such cognitive biases being present reduces the chance that they will operate in our work with our client with SUD and that if they do occur, we will more readily address them, thereby meeting the "North Star Guide."

The author of this text makes specific recommendations for the use of creative techniques in working with an SUD population in Box 3D.

BOX 3D: MILLER'S RECOMMENDATIONS FOR THE USE OF CREATIVE TECHNIQUES

- Be aware of the different impact on people with SUD individually.
- Expect to spend more time processing: Multiply expected time for an activity by 3 (e.g., 10-minute exercise taking 30 minutes).
- Make sure they feel safe: Set up rules for safety.
- Closely observe their verbal and nonverbal reactions to techniques in order to determine how the technique is impacting them.
- Make sure that they have time to process their reactions and stop the session if there is a powerful reaction to the technique or they look like they are feeling unsafe.
- Take care of the "traumatized child" within them by guiding them on calming themselves through their senses.

For more specific recommendations connected to one's professional orientation, it is suggested that the reader contact their professional organization and view any recommendations they have for the employment of creative techniques in their practice.

"Limits" is a relative term. Like beauty, it is often in the eye of the beholder.

—Chris Burden, experimental performance artist and sculptor

Specific Creative Techniques

Story/Metaphor

The use of the techniques of story and metaphor by the helping professional can assist the SUD person in recalling the content being conveyed in the session. These include stories and metaphors told by the helping professional, those shared by other SUD persons in a group setting, as well as stories and metaphors shared by the SUD person themselves.

Personal Recovery Story

[Alcohol] makes me forget. It's a disease that keeps saying I have no disease.

—Mariette Hartley, actor (as quoted in Stromberg & Merrill, 2005, p.163)

The Story Behind the Statement

Mariette Hartley grew up in the 1940s in an "artistic, hard-drinking, alcoholic community" (Stromberg & Merrill, 2005, p. 152). She described both of her parents as alcoholic and mentally ill: Her father was manic-depressive, and her mother was also manic-depressive or depressed. She watched her father have delirium tremens and her parents fight and have blackouts. She had one brother who was 15 months younger. Her father adored her and they understood each other's creativity, while her mother did not. She described herself as a creative person that was restrained by her environment and controlled by her mother's guilting of her. She described her family as a family of secrets. At age 12, her maternal grandfather, "a famous behavioral psychologist, a man named John B. Watson, who believed that children should not be touched or held" (Stromberg & Merrill, 2005, p. 156), French-kissed her. She started drinking at age 14 with a boyfriend who drank alcoholically. She was sexual in high school and drank to handle her shame and guilt about her sexuality. She never enjoyed drinking, but as a closet drinker, she used it to anesthetize her pain as she had watched her family do. She married at age 19 after dating her husband for 3 weeks and was married 2 years. She stated she was physically abused in the marriage. Under the pressure of her mother, she aborted her first pregnancy. She later had a son and a daughter with her second husband, a

French man who drank champagne and wine, who she had supported financially throughout their marriage.

Over time she realized she needed to divorce her husband; her sobriety was hard on her marriage. She and her parents moved in together in Hollywood. Her maternal grandfather, who they visited frequently, lived near them. Her father, who had PTSD from WWII, killed himself in their home with a shotgun, and her drinking became worse. She returned to school and studied psychology and philosophy after his death. She had ADHD, drank alcohol, and was bulimic during this time. In this time frame, she 1(a) went into therapy to break out of her enmeshed, codependent relationship with her mother, (b) cofounded the American Foundation for Suicide Prevention in the 1980s in response to her father's death, and (c) went into 12-step recovery after attending a meeting and experiencing a desire to have what they had, as expressed in their eyes. She describes herself being obsessed with drinking and acted as a "good daughter" in support groups where she gave to others but did not ask for what she needed. She relapsed. She sobered up in Jamaica, and when she returned to America, she obtained a therapist with whom she shared her life story and began to heal. She found that telling her story of alcoholism and child abuse was healing for her, although it was hard on her mother, and she began to tell her story in writing and speaking (e.g., recovery groups, prisons). Her mother died shortly after her book about her life, *Breaking the Silence*, was published; she died in her arms. She described her sobriety as powerful and eclectic journey where she surrendered to "the Light" (Stromberg & Merrill, 2005, p. 164) and has been able to maintain sobriety. She stated that it is a struggle for those in recovery, such as herself, to accept success in life (e.g., relationships). She had a spiritual advisor in her recovery who told her, "One's deepest wounds, integrated, become one's greatest powers" (Stromberg & Merrill, 2005, p. 164).

The actor found that by finding a creative way of telling her story of substance abuse and trauma (e.g., writing, speaking), she began to heal in her recovery. Having others "hear" her story through her writings and presentations assisted them in their healing process. The use of story and metaphor in our work with the SUD population, then, may be a powerful avenue of healing in their SUD recovery as well as those who hear their story.

REVIEW OF THE LITERATURE

The research supports the effectiveness for both telling one's story (e.g., storytelling, writing) and the use of metaphor.

Storytelling/writing is an effective technique helping professionals can use with their clients with SUD. This technique

- facilitates happiness and resilience (Moghadam, et al., 2016), messages of hope and recovery (Judd et al., 2023; Paterno et al., 2018), and meaning of sobriety and identity (Wulbert, 2018);
- assists in overcoming stigma (Barton, 2019; Judd et al., 2023; Williams, 2023);
- increases self-esteem, stress response, and insight (Barton, 2019; Park & Kim, 2023);
- assists the client/patient in rewriting their life story (Barton, 2019; Clark, 2014; Ricks et al., 2014); and
- facilitates emotional healing (Barton, 2019; Davidson, 2020).

Because the goal is to help the person with SUD to feel safe as they tell their story and focus on telling their recovery story, some specific questions that may assist the person with SUD in the telling of the story are outlined in Appendix 3A at the end of this chapter.

As a technique, *metaphor* can assist the person with SUD:

- understand their issues related to their substance use through words/phrases provided by the health professional (e.g., "liquid handcuffs" for methadone that helps them have "money in their pockets"; Malvini Redden et al., 2013)
- decrease their stigma and shame (Gul & Aqeel, 2021)

Storytelling (metaphor) can also assist in the reduction of negative affect and feelings when there is difficulty in the therapy relationship.

Both storytelling and the use of metaphor may be beneficial techniques that can be employed with clients with SUD. If integrating storytelling and the use of metaphor with their work, the reader needs to remember to practice within one's area of competence . If the helping professional is not trained in this area, the approach taken needs to be careful, flexible, and adaptable in terms of their own unique role, setting, and SUD client population. This means that the helping professional

- integrates storytelling and the use of metaphor into the therapeutic relationship they have with their client/patient (e.g., individual, couple, family, group);
- stops the storytelling and the use of metaphor techniques and, if contraindications occur, processes the reaction with the client/patient; and
- works closely/consults with other professionals about using storytelling and the use of metaphor techniques in our professional work given our role, setting, and client population.

The "one" that I am is composed of narratives that overlap,
run parallel to and often contradict one another.

—*Glenn Ligon, painter*

Humor

The use of the technique of humor by the helping professional can also assist the SUD person in recalling the content being conveyed in the session. This section discusses different ways humor may be used or encouraged in sessions in addition to specific nuances related to the use of humor.

Personal Recovery Story

[My friends] took me to an ER where the doctor recognized
me. ... He said, "Richard, what are you doing?" I said, "I'm
killing myself, but no more. I quit. I can't beat this disease."
And that was it.

—*Richard Lewis, comedian/writer/ actor (quoted in*
Stromberg & Merrill, 2005, p. 225)

The Story Behind the Statement

Richard Lewis had an older brother and sister and was born into the Jewish religion. In his interview for the book *The Harder They Fall* (Stromberg & Merrill, 2005), he described his father as a workaholic who was a great caterer and his mother as a hypochondriacal, narcissistic woman who had low self-esteem, felt guilty about everything, and was hard on him. He stated her lack of loving nurturance resulted in his need to fill the emptiness inside of him with praise and applause as well as the affection of women. His sister moved away from home when he was 8, and his older brother had issues that he needed to address. He reported that he felt misunderstood, unappreciated, and invalidated by important people in his life because of their problems. In college, he discovered that by doing stand-up comedy he could get a natural high from making people laugh. Upon college graduation, he became a comedy writer. Besides a natural high, writing and performing comedy had brought him a natural way to express himself. When his father died when he was 23, he described an emptiness inside of him. After his death, writing jokes was not enough for him, so he began to perform comedy. Even though it took him 10–15 years to make a decent living off of it, he enjoyed performing comedy. However, he felt judged whenever he went on stage, and he found that in this environment that had a lot of alcohol, drinking helped him relax, celebrate, avoid issues, handle negative criticism, and decrease his negative feelings.

In *The Harder They Fall* (Stromberg & Merrill, 2005), Lewis described his early 40s as being controlled by his need to drink alcohol. During his alcohol use, he also used cocaine. He quit stand-up comedy at the height of his career because, in his words, he believed he would make a mess of it. He decided to begin acting, where he continued to drink either when alone or when he was dating women. After a friend coordinated an intervention for him in his hotel room with other friends and his sister present, he went to a doctor and was referred to rehab. He spent one night and a morning in rehab and then left because he felt humiliated, out of control, and ashamed in relation to his being a celebrity. The day after leaving, he went to a self-help group in Los Angeles and has attended self-help groups since that time. He had two relapses since beginning self-help groups and stated he does not know their cause. He described how 3 months after being in rehab he went to the emergency room and hit his bottom, as described in the opening statement. He said his mother never believed he was alcoholic because she felt responsible for it. She died 4½ years into his recovery. He wrote a book that he stated is essentially about his life, *The Other Great Depression*. He said that in order to be sober, a person needs to be sober, want to be sober, and have courage and faith. He said that while it may be hard for him to experience his feelings in their entirety sober, the benefit in his recovery is that he can trust his feelings and be clear about them. He says he believes that he is a very spiritual (not religious) person and he believes that God is everywhere. At the end of his interview, he said he wanted to leave a legacy of helping others who are addicted turn their lives around.

The story of Richard Lewis demonstrates how we simply love people who make us laugh (Dayton, 2007). As a comedian, stand-up comedy initially helped him relax and have his need for connection with others met through his engagement with his audience. Regarding comedians (as well as humorists), Daniel L. Araoz, diplomate in clinical hypnosis, family therapy, and counseling psychology, stated in an interview, "The humorist, like a comedian, helps us see more of a reality or look at it from a different perspective. This is an enrichment of our life. Thomas Aquinas, in the Middle Ages, considered it a virtue to make other people laugh" (Goldin et al., 2006, p. 397).

Lewis's type of humor been labeled *performance humor*, which is humor "produced mainly by people who make their living on humor … television-sitcoms, stand-up comedy, humorous books and movies" (Martin & Kuiper, 2016, p. 508). This type of humor can be viewed as "a sort of 'stand-in' for the conversational humor that occurs in everyday life" (Martin & Kuiper, 2016, p. 508). *Conversational humor* refers to "everyday joke-telling, humorous personal anecdotes, witty banter, irony, and other funny comments that tend to occur spontaneously in all sorts of social interactions" (Martin & Kuiper, 2016, p. 507). Conversational humor may be more pertinent for emotional and physical health and well-being (Martin & Kuiper, 2016).

The exchange of healing between individuals as they laugh is noted by Ackerman (1970/1982) who writes about the power of laughter in the context of mental health therapy: "Nothing releases like a hearty laugh. It eases the jangled nerves of everyone, including the therapist. It releases tension, gives pleasure, enhances rapport, rewards openness and honesty, facilitates the uncovering of relevant emotions, and heightens the efficacy of the opening" (p. 286).

According to Dixon (1980), "Humor may have evolved as a uniquely human strategy for coping with stress" (as cited in Martin & Lefcourt, 1983, p. 1313). Overall, humor, which is universal, begins early in our lives (about 4 months of age) and is woven into the fabric of our lives as we interact with others through various social contexts (e.g., therapy, education, workplace; Canha, 2020; Martin, 2007; Martin & Kuiper, 2016). Human beings are social animals who need healthy personal relationships (both close relationships and casual) that impact our psychological health, and humor is a part of those relationship inter-actions (Martin & Kuiper, 2016). Paradoxically, then, because of the depth and breadth of its presence in our lives, it is necessary for helping professionals to take humor seriously.

REVIEW OF THE LITERATURE

The review of the literature is a combination of research conducted with general populations and specific populations related to helping professional clients (e.g., mental health, medical, SUD). As humor relates to psychotherapy, a historical review of its use has been sum-marized by Martin and Lefcourt (1983):

- Freud (1959, 1960) viewed humor as the highest defense mechanism—a coping mechanism that is adaptive.
- Allport (1950) stated that being able to laugh at oneself may assist in enhanced self-management.
- May (1953) described humor as assisting with self-preservation because of its capacity to assist a person in distancing themselves from their problem and seeing it from a different perspective.

In spite of its historical roots in the history of psychotherapy and support for the use of humor both theoretically and clinically, there is limited research on humor in psychotherapy (Sultanoff, 2013). Even so, within these limitations, the following points are known about humor:

- Humor is used for different purposes at different times and in different contexts (Martin, 2007).
- Culture impacts how humor is used and what humor is appro-priate (Martin, 2007).
- Humor may improve life quality and satisfaction (Canha, 2020, 2016; Martin, 2007).
- Humor's psychological functions include (a) cognitive and social benefits, (b) enhanced social communication and influence, and (c) tension relief, emotional regulation, and enhanced stress coping (Canha, 2020, 2016; Martin, 2007; Martin & Kuiper, 2016; Martin & Lefcourt, 1983; Sultanoff, 2013; Taylor, 2023).

The benefits of the use of humor can be divided into short-term and long-term benefits (Martin, 2007; Martin & Kuiper, 2016). *Short-term benefits* include an enhanced feeling of well-being; an increased sense of mastery/control; a decrease in negative emotions (e.g., anxiety, helplessness, depression, anger); and a reduction of impairments (emotional, physiological, behavioral) due to stressful life experiences. For example, humor results in greater physiological and emotional well-being (Buerger & Miller, 2022; Martin & Kuiper, 2016) and as provides relief in the moment (Martin & Kuiper, 2016; Sultanoff, 2013). *Long-term benefits* depend on how individuals use humor daily and is related to the type of humor used as well as the type of humor *not used*. Healthy long-term benefits are experienced if people use humor in a manner that is sensitive to their own needs and that of others. Those benefits are increased self-esteem, emotional well-being, and more satisfying relationships. However, if humor is used to enhance one's own emotions and stress reduction at another's expense (e.g., sarcasm, teasing), the long-term unhealthy results can be a humor backlash that expresses itself in interpersonal problems and alienation.

In an interview conducted with Martin (Martin & Kuiper, 2016), three major components of humor occurring in social, interpersonal contexts were presented:

- **Cognitive:** This refers to the "perception of incongruity" (p. 502) as experienced by the individual.
- **Emotional:** The cognitive processes result in an activation of an emotional response (e.g., mirth). *Mirth* is like joy in that it activates the limbic system pleasure circuits and the autonomic and endocrine responses.
- **Social/interpersonal:** Typically occurring in small groups, this component involves laughter. *Laughter* is the "hard-wired nonverbal expression or communication of the emotion of mirth (p. 502).

When discussing the use of humor in relation to the clinical work of mental health counselors (that can readily be applied to health professionals in general), Martin (Martin & Kuiper, 2016) makes three suggestions: First, be aware of how clients use (and can use) humor in their lives. Second, be aware of how humor can be used in the therapeutic relationship. Third, be aware of how maladaptive humor can be a part of the client's dysfunction. For example, more adaptive humor with partners can increase a sense of intimacy and positive moods and thus result in greater relationship satisfaction.

When we have an alliance with and know the person, humor can enhance a feeling of closeness in the helping relationship (Goldin et al., 2006; Martin, 2007; Sultanoff, 2013). The platform on which the helping professional can use the technique of humor consists of three theories regarding humor. Each theory may operate separately or simultaneously as they are expressed in humor that is used in the helping relationship. These theories are:

- **Arousal:** This theory views humor as a "complex mind–body interaction of cognition and emotion that is rooted in the biological substrates of our brain and nervous system" (Martin, 2007, p. 82). For example, the interaction results in physical benefits such as relaxation. Also, humor and laughter positively impact biochemistry (e.g., laughter causes levels of stress hormones to decrease and levels of antibodies to increase; Sultanoff, 2013) and increase the levels of adrenaline, noradrenaline, and cortisol levels by activating the sympathetic-adrenal-medullary system (Martin, 2007). Canha (2020), in application of the theory to the SUD population diagnosed with opioid use disorder (OUD), states that humor, as an intervention, stimulates the reward center of the brain, releasing dopamine. Clients with an active SUD do not enjoy the natural rewards of food, sex, and humor, but those in recovery enjoy these natural rewards again, especially humor (Canha, 2020). With the SUD population, then, health professionals can use various interventions (e.g., stand-up comedy, comedy movies, comedy television shows, recovery-related cartoons, jokes) to disrupt affect, cognition, and behavior, resulting in the reward center of the brain being stimulated (Canha, 2020).
- **Incongruity:** From this theoretical perspective, humor invites the examination of two or more incongruous, incompatible perspectives simultaneously of people, situations, and events (Martin & Kuiper, 2016). When the health professional uses humor in this manner, the technique may help the client with SUD learn to tolerate ambivalence and look at the situation from an amusing, comical perspective (Canha, 2020; Dayton, 2007). This allows them some helpful emotional distance from the situation (Martin & Kuiper, 2016).
- **Reversal:** In this theory, humor is a form of play where we enjoy incongruities in our interactions with others. Examples of this include "jokes, nonverbal humor, conversational witticisms, and

the humorous outlook on the adversities of life that forms the basis of humor as a coping mechanism" (Martin, 2007, p. 82). Again, this can be used by the health professional to assist the person with SUD in living in their recovery in terms of simply having fun, feeling good, being playful, and sharing laughter in their supportive social interactions (e.g., Narcotics Anonymous).

In employing humor as a technique, considerations of its use include (Goldin et al., 2006; Sultanoff, 2013):

- timing
- appropriateness
- receptivity
- the possibility of offending the person (e.g., being disrespectful, trivializing the problem, showing "bad taste")

Canha (2020) states that in terms of consideration of the use of humor with the client with OUD, if the person is new to recovery, they may be sensitive to humor and easily view themselves as being the target of the joke. Therefore, employing humor needs to be adapted to the individual in order to determine if the approaches are appropriate. For example, Sultanoff (2013) describes mental health clients who have rigid thinking and an inactive sense of humor as possibly being resistant to humor in the helping relationship. Additionally, this author suggests that the safest form of the use of humor is, when appropriate, the SUD helping professional making a joke about themselves. The author also encourages the reader to assist the client with SUD in finding a balance with humor so they are not using it, as the comedian did, to avoid addressing their issues or go to the other extreme of having no sense of humor.

Contraindications for the use of the technique in the helping relationship can readily be applied to working with the SUD population (Goldin et al., 2006; Sultanoff, 2013):

- unreadiness of the individual for humor
- the individual not seeing humor as appropriate
- humor potentially harming the alliance
- humor potentially harming the person

Also, Sultanoff (2013) cautions mental health therapists that the use of humor in therapy is a greater risk than in other relationships because of the trust in the therapist that increases their vulnerability to emotional harm. This caution may apply to health professionals in general and particularly those working with clients with SUD who are early in their recovery process and thus may be very sensitive to humor, as noted by Canha (2020).

When applied to the helping relationship, the technique of humor may be helpful in these ways:

- being in the present moment (Goldin et al., 2006)
- facilitating communication (Canha, 2020; Goldin et al., 2006)
- increasing the sense of being understood (Canha, 2020; Goldin et al., 2006)
- holding attention (Buerger et al., 2022; Goldin et al., 2006)
- making topics more interesting (e.g., they can learn principles of recovery; Canha, 2020, 2016; Goldin et al., 2006)
- lowering defenses, allowing them to learn more readily (Dayton, 2007; Sultanoff, 2013) and thereby impacting memory and learning (Berger et al., 2022; Canha, 2020; Sultanoff, 2013)
- changing perceptions of the situation, emotional state, and relationships (Canha, 2020; Martin, 2007; Martin & Kuiper, 2016; Sultanoff, 2013)
- seeing the absurdity of the world (Canha, 2020; Goldin et al., 2006; Sultanoff, 2013) and thus enhancing adaptations (Canha, 2020; Martin, 2007; Martin & Kuiper, 2016; Sultanoff, 2013)
- reframing problems so they see them in a more positive light and not take them so seriously (Canha, 2020; Goldin et al., 2006; Martin & Kuiper, 2016; Sultanoff, 2013)

In summary, humor, when used appropriately, is a powerful, useful technique in the helping relationship with clients with SUD, helping them learn how to live, reframe their problems in a positive manner, and change their behaviors (Canha, 2020). Further exploration regarding humor with clients with SUD can be facilitated by the helping professional through self-examination questions. An example of such questions that can be used to explore how they experience humor are presented in Appendix 3A at the end of this chapter.

Humor and laughter—not necessarily derogatory derision—are my pet tools.

—Marcel Duchamp, painter, sculptor, chess player, and writer

Experiential Activity/Play

Assisting in session content recall by the SUD person is the use of the techniques of experiential activity and play by the helping professional. Experiential activities and play invite the SUD person to be engaged in the session rather than being distracted or reticent to interact.

Personal Recovery Story

I needed drugs to do certain things and alcohol to do other things. ... Drugs got me in a lot of trouble in baseball and in the press. ... The first person I met in treatment was ... a psychologist who told me I was suicidal. I told him he was a damn fool. ... He told me that anyone that would take all this stuff [commenting on a drug list I had given him] is trying to kill themselves. Right then I said, "You don't ever have to worry about me and drugs and alcohol again, 'cause I ain't no damn fool." That's all it took for me to get it. That was it! ... I know that if I ever use again, I'll kill myself, and that's the bottom line.

*—Dock Ellis, professional baseball pitcher
(quoted in Stromberg & Merrill, 2005, pp. 59–60)*

The Story Behind the Statement

Dock Ellis was born to parents who did not drink; his grandfather drank brewed beer and vodka ("boilermakers"). He started drinking vodka at age 3 because he thought it was water, and his parents found him drunk in the basement (they thought he was asleep). He said he always drank alcohol, and while his sisters knew he was drinking, his parents did not. His father was always gone because he was in the hospital a lot, and his mother just thought Dock drank a lot. When his father lost an $800,000 bet, the family had to move to Watts in Los Angeles. It was then that he started using marijuana in order to fit into his peer group. When he began competing in sports (e.g., basketball, football), he began mixing wine with the barbiturate Seconal ("red devils"). He played as a baseball pitcher in the minor and major leagues from 1964–1979 after signing up to play baseball in 1963 upon release from jail for car theft. He said baseball allowed him to meet many people, travel, and provided him with numerous opportunities (e.g., jobs in the movies).

Dock became heavily involved with drugs when he went to the major leagues. He described himself as a functioning baseball player even though he was addicted to alcohol and drugs (e.g., amphetamines) that messed up his game. An example of this is when he pitched a no-hitter when high on acid in 1970; he had taken the acid because it was supposed to have been his day off. His dad encouraged him in baseball whether he lost (provided encouragement) or he won (celebrated with him). In 1965 his dad died, and he began using cocaine. When he played with the Pittsburgh Pirates, he was well liked. He said he found it hard to deal with the press daily because of an antagonistic relationship between them. He went to treatment because friends told him he had a problem and he did not want to hurt his infant son. After treatment, he lost his son through a divorce and he went back to school to become a substance abuse counselor. When his son was 14, they reconnected and stayed connected since that time. He worked as a substance abuse counselor, with most of his professional life spent working in correctional facilities. His sobriety date was September 30, 1980.

(Note: Dock Ellis died in 2008 and the "Story Behind the Statement" is based on his interview for the book *The Harder They Fall* [Stromberg & Merrill, 2005].)

Another baseball player, Lou Gehrig, stated in his farewell speech ("baseball's Gettysburg Address") on July 4, 1939, regarding his year's playing baseball, "I have been in ballparks for 17 years. ... I might have been given a bad break [in terms of his health], but I've got an awful lot to live for" (Quercus, 2006, p. 96). This statement reflects the similarity between Lou Gehrig and Dock Ellis in that they both loved baseball and played it for many years. In contrast, Dock Ellis's playing became fused with his substance use, resulting in them having different outcomes with the press (e.g., negative ones for Ellis) and negative consequences in Ellis's life both personally and professionally. In this section, the positive power of play (that was present throughout Gehrig's career and only initially present in Ellis's experience in his first year before substance use entered into his professional life) is explored as a technique that can be used as helping professionals assist the resilience of the recovering person with SUD through encouragement.

Play, like humor, is universal and begins early in our lives. Two examples of that are elucidated here. First, at about age 2, *pretend play* (also known as *make believe*) begins. Here children take on roles and mimic others in terms of their actions and characteristics as they socially interact with other children (Broderick & Blewitt, 2020). Second, toddlers/preschoolers engage in *exploratory play* where they spontaneously use objects and learn about object properties and spatial/numerical/categorical relations (Broderick & Blewitt, 2020). Through play they learn mind skills that include the perspectives of others (Broderick & Blewitt, 2020). Play helps strengthen "imagination, cooperation, flexibility, imitation of adult roles and enriched language use" (Broderick & Blewitt, 2020, p. 115). As Walsh (2008) stated about his play with Wham-O toys (e.g., SuperBalls, Frisbee, Hula-Hoop) as a child, "I discovered things while at play."(p. 3) This learning can be facilitated by adults and teachers (preschool, elementary). For readers who work with children, they may find the Association for Play Therapy (APT; https://a4pt.org), an organization that focuses on play therapy with children, to be helpful in their work. Because play, like humor, begins early in life and has a significant impact throughout our lives, it needs to be examined as a technique with adolescents and adults who struggle with SUD.

As with children, people with SUD (e.g., adolescents, adults) can engage in pretend play where they take on roles and mimic others (e.g., role-play) during sessions with the helping professional in couples, family, or group sessions in order to learn about themselves. For example, a person with SUD may benefit from role-playing their partner, who is concerned about their use, in order to view the impact of their use on another person. An example of exploratory play for the person with SUD may involve their using objects that may be considered toys that they played with as a child or ones they can learn to play with (e.g., SuperBalls, Frisbee, Hula-Hoop; Walsh, 2008). As they did as children, they may make self-discoveries through the use of such objects.

Play may, as noted in the section on humor, involve

- cultural impact (e.g., how play occurs and what is considered appropriate);
- improvement in life quality and satisfaction; and
- psychological benefits regarding connection, social communication/influence, and tension relief/emotional regulation/enhanced stress coping.

As with humor, timing, appropriateness, receptivity, and possibly offending the client with SUD (e.g., disrespecting them, trivializing the clinical work, showing poor taste) need to be considered. It is also necessary that the client with SUD feels free to join or not join in play (Dayton, 2007). Again, contraindications for inclusion of play in sessions may include the person with SUD is not ready, it is not appropriate, it will hurt the working alliance, or it harms the person.

Many of the ways humor can be helpful to the person with SUD that were listed in the humor section can possibly be applied to play. For example, play can assist the person with SUD live in the moment and hold their attention. It may be a way they learn new ways to have fun (besides using substances) or rediscover ways they had fun prior to their substance use. In participating in such activities, either in or away from their session with the helping professional, they can (a) experience the awkwardness of participating in these activities sober and (b) change their perception of themselves, their recovery, their emotions, and their relationships. The overall goal is to assist the person with SUD in learning how to enjoy life without the use of substances.

One such helpful approach can be the provision of role models of play for the person with SUD, such as the river otter. According to Jenkins (1998), the river otter is the most playful of animals in the water. If, for example, the otter cannot play when doing something, it does not appear to be something it considers worthwhile to do. Also, while play with other otters is preferred, the individual otter can play alone for long periods of time (Jenkins, 1998). An example of this type may help the person with SUD understand the importance of integrating play into their lives whenever possible and that play can be with others or alone—both of which may be new concepts for the person with SUD.

However, play, possibly even more so than humor, may have childish connotations, as well as being difficult to define. Viewing it as childish may create barriers to its incorporation in the recovery of the client with SUD. In terms of definition, there may be different kinds of play: competitive (either with self or others) or play where few rules (if any) are involved. Additionally, the experience of play, while it involves a sense of novelty and open-endedness, is idiosyncratically defined for each person with SUD: What is play to one person is stressful for another person (e.g., crossword puzzles) or is viewed as silly or serious (e.g., blowing bubbles; using a Hula-Hoop). Also, for the person with SUD who is prone to extremes, overall reactions to the form of play may be polarized by extremes of a rigidity against it or an extreme inclusion of it.

As with the section on humor, further exploration regarding play (having fun) with the person with SUD can be facilitated by the helping professional through self-examination questions. An example of such questions that can be used to explore how they play sober is presented in Appendix 3A at the end of this chapter.

As stated in the section on humor, paradoxically, because of the depth and breadth of play as a presence in our lives, it is necessary for helping professionals to take play seriously.

REVIEW OF THE LITERATURE

As a tendency, adults spend too little time in play even though play encourages positive emotions (e.g., smiles, laughter), autonomy, spontaneity, creativity, and relationships where we learn about each other, share mutual interests, and become closer (Dayton, 2007). Play, for adults as well as children, results in our letting our guards down and allowing ourselves to be silly (Heiden, 2008). However, with adults, there is a stigma to adults playing, and play (e.g., toys, games) is different for adults. When children play, the play is separate from the child's life, whereas when adults play, the play is often imbedded in activities that are productive and purposeful (e.g., stress management; Heiden, 2008). An example of imbedded play activities is the use of TikTok videos developed by individuals with SUD to both increase their recovery support as well as share hope with others struggling with SUD as they enjoy the activity of developing a video (Russell et al., 2021).

In terms of play therapy with adults, Heiden (2008) makes a number of points:

- There is not much research on adult play therapy.
- Play therapy is not aligned with a specific theory; rather, it is imbedded in existing theories of counseling (e.g., Gestalt, Adlerian, client-centered).
- The goal of play therapy is to create a safe environment for addressing intense issues and form relationships (e.g., alliance between the helping professional and the client/patient) that allow expression of thoughts and feelings.
- Play therapy enhances comfort in sessions and encourages a less formal exploration of issues.

- The experiential aspect (the metaphor of play) facilitates the healing process by helping adults (especially trauma survivors) communicate about their issues.
- Play therapy is useful with adults to experiment with roles, learn new skills, and create/recreate their life events as well as consider their dilemma from a new perspective.

In summary, whether the helping professional encourages play in the recovery of a client with SUD or incorporates play (experiential activities) into sessions, it has the potential of a powerful impact on the SUD recovery work that is happening between the helping professional and the client with SUD.

I don't know where I'm going, but I'll get there on time.

—*Robert Rauschenberg, painter and graphic artist*

Music

The use of music as a technique by the helping professional can assist the SUD person in recalling the content being conveyed in the session. This section discusses different ways to use music in sessions as well as different purposes for the use of music.

Personal Recovery Story

Around two weeks later [in a 12-step treatment program], I ran into Chuck [who had driven me from jail to the treatment center], and he said, "How you doing?" And I said, "Well, I'm not in jail." And he said, "You know what? You don't have to be, ever again."

I realized I never wanted to be in jail again. …
I started listening to people [in the treatment center].

—*Steve Earle, musician (quoted in Stromberg & Merrill, 2005, p. 245)*

The Story Behind the Statement

Steve Earle started drinking at age 11 or 12 because everybody around him drank and used drugs in the late 1960s and early 1970s. He especially liked LSD and heroin (e.g., he did not even throw up the first time he shot up heroin). It was his uncle, who was 5 years older than him, who introduced him to his first drugs.

In his late teens, alcohol became his core drug, and he was caught in the physical addiction to heroin a number of times in high school but was able to withdraw off it on his own. At 19 he moved to Tennessee where there was little heroin and he focused on using alcohol and marijuana; he quite the latter substance because he experienced anxiety attacks and paranoia. Due to the prevalence of cocaine in Nashville in the mid 1970s, as a songwriter he resumed his use of cocaine (even though he knew how addictive it was from when he had used it previously in his youth).

He married five times, with his substance use impacting his marriages. His first marriage ended due to his drug use and his involvement with the woman who became his second wife. His second wife used drugs like he did; however, he stopped using cocaine because of a frightening anxiety attack he had when free-basing cocaine. When he stopped using cocaine, his second marriage ended, and at the end of that marriage, he quit using substances completely until he met his third wife who worked in a bar, and then he began drinking beer. During that time, he also started taking prescription opiates and liked them. In the 1980s, he started making records (releasing his first major album in 1986) and continued to use opiates a lot. Over the course of his substance use, he entered methadone programs twice for his opiate use. He left his fourth wife, who he describes as a "codependent" that he deeply loved, after she participated in an intervention on him. They later remarried.

His substance use began to impact his work as a musician; for example, he could not write a film soundtrack that he had agreed to write. He also began to have legal problems (e.g., conflicts with the police, forgetting about a sentencing hearing). He decided to turn himself in to the police after he used crack cocaine one last time. It was during this jail time that he was allowed to go to a 12-step treatment center; he paid for his own detox at a county hospital.

He went to treatment to get out of jail, not to become sober, and he planned to use substances when he completed treatment until his encounter with Chuck described in the opening quote. After this encounter, he realized he did not want to go to jail again and, as he describes it, accepted responsibility for why he was in jail, stopped seeing himself as a victim, and started listening to people at the treatment center.

He was in treatment for 28 days and then returned to jail where substances were available, but instead of using substances, during his remaining 4½ months in jail, he attended 12-step meetings and remained sober. At the time of his interview, he attended 12-step meetings daily in Nashville and when on tour.

(Note: This "Story Behind the Statement" is based on an interview with Steve Earle in the book *The Harder They Fall* [Stromberg & Merrill, 2005].)

As with the, musician's story, music may (a) be paired with substance use and (b) provide the musician with a connection with the audience. We, the audience, pair music with experiences we have when we hear it, *if* the music "touches" us. For example, a song may take us back to a time and place where we felt loved and help us forget about our current struggles as we remember that loving experience. However, the same song we hear at another time may take us to grief because an important relationship ended for us and the song causes us to remember our grief. Music's connection with others is evidenced in the following quote: "A painter paints pictures on canvas, but musicians paint their pictures on silence. We provide the music, and you provide the silence" (Leopold Stokowski addressing an audience at Carnegie Hall; as quoted in Big Think, 2014).

REVIEW OF THE LITERATURE

Music therapy (MT) and music-based interventions (MBIs) are being used with an increasing frequency with the SUD population even though its efficacy is unclear (American Music Therapy Association [AMTA], 2021; Carter et al., 2021; Hohmann et al., 2017). This means that we know music therapy is helpful to SUD clients/patients (AMTA, 2021), but we are not sure as to how/why it is helpful. There is a lack of demonstrated significant results and significant researcher bias as well as being conducted typically in single-sessions and on detox units (AMTA, 2021). At the same time, in qualitative studies, clients/patients show a preference for music therapy as a part of their SUD treatment (AMTA, 2021).

Musical experiences in SUD treatment include:

- music listening (e.g., song discussion)
- lyric analysis*
- songwriting*
- music assisted creative arts
- music assisted mediation (e.g., guided imagery)
- active music-making (AMTA, 2021, p. 2)

*These experiences are noted as the most commonly used music therapy interventions in addition to recreational music therapy (Silverman, 2022). *Recreational music therapy* is sometimes called *music therapy games* that increase the likelihood of client/patient participation and returning to music therapy sessions. Examples of these include music trivia, music charades, and musical chairs (Silverman, 2022).

The American Music Therapy Association (AMTA; 2021) comments on the use of music in the SUD population. First, music can be a part of an integrated SUD treatment and used in the context of the therapeutic relationship. For example, because it has been shown to activate dopaminergic pathways in a similar manner to alcohol/drugs (Bourdaghs et al., 2020), music therapy can be used as an alternative experience of "getting high" that does not involve substances. Also, music can engage them in treatment (Carter & Panisch, 2021; Dingle et al., 2008; Silverman, 2022). Second, it may benefit clients by (a) promoting connection within themselves and motivating them to stay sober; (b) reducing cravings and improving mood; and (c) encouraging relaxation and decreasing anxiety. Regarding the third benefit, music therapy helps them break out of regular, harmful, and painful emotional patterns (Soshensky, 2001), such as depression (Carter & Panisch, 2021; Situmorang, 2020) anxiety (Situmorang, 2020), and stress (Situmorang, 2020). It has been used with specific populations (e.g., women) and has shown they experience an improvement in their mood (e.g., reduced anxiety), enjoyment, self-sense, and energy (Gardstrom & Diestelkamp, 2013; Gardstrom et al., 2017). Third, music may be contraindicated because it triggers trauma and/or substance use and increases cravings for substances.

The caution to the reader is to remember to practice within one's area of competence; if a helping professional wants to integrate music with their work but is not trained in music therapy, they must be careful, flexible, and adaptable in their approach and thoughtfully apply it to their own unique role, setting, and SUD client population. This means that we (Miller, 2023):

- Integrate music into the therapeutic relationship we have with our client/patient (e.g., individual, couple, family, group).
- Stop the music and process what has happened with our client/patient if contraindications occur, as this can provide an opportunity to teach our clients the skills that are being used in the session (e.g., deep breathing) can be used outside the setting if they experience a contraindication to the music.
- Work closely/consult with a music therapist about using music in our professional work given our role, setting, and client population. Appendix 3A at the end of this chapter contains general and specific *questions* (adapted from Miller, 2023) that can be asked of SUD persons. An MI approach with the questions is encouraged to draw out the client's reactions to the music.

Gardstrom (2021) provides additional questions that the helping professional can present to their client/patient to answer:

1. What specific music stimuli might trigger my cravings?
2. What personal strategies might help me to manage my music-induced cravings?
   o WHAT music might be best for me to listen to/avoid?
   o WHEN should I listen to music/avoid listening to music?
   o WHERE should I listen to music/avoid listening to music?
   o HOW should I listen to music?

Box 3E (adapted from Miller, 2023) contains specific music techniques that can be adapted to any clinical format (e.g., individual, couple, family, group).

BOX 3E: SPECIFIC MUSIC TECHNIQUES THAT CAN BE ADAPTED TO ANY CLINICAL FORMAT

1. Have the client/patient play their favorite music (e.g., song) from when they were using and process their reactions.
2. Have them play their favorite music (e.g., song) that helps them stay sober and encourages them to have hope.
3. Give them assignments to listen to music that helps them:
   o feel more connected to themselves ("I feel okay.")
   o motivates them to stay sober ("I can do this.")
   o helps them relax and be less anxious ("I am safe in the world.")

SUMMARY

In this chapter, three areas were reviewed: (a) the four-legged stool self-care framework that encourages a balanced recovery lifestyle, (b) creative technique guidelines that invite healing and avoid harm in the person with SUD, and (c) specific creative techniques in four specific areas: story and metaphor; humor; experiential activity and play; and music. In summary, four specific areas of creative techniques (story and metaphor; humor; experiential activity and play; music) were reviewed in this chapter. This information can be a resource for the reader of techniques that can be adapted to their specific SUD population.

KEY POINTS

1. The four-legged stool self-care framework was presented. The framework is designed to help the person with SUD develop a balanced recovery lifestyle that assists them in the short- and long-term maintenance of their recovery.
2. Guidelines for the use of creative techniques were discussed because of their ability to both harm and heal the person with SUD. The potential power of these techniques to harm or heal rests on their ability to "bypass" the defense structures of the person with SUD.
3. Specific creative techniques were reviewed in four of the creative arts areas (story/metaphor; humor; experiential activity/play; music). In relation to SUD, each area included a person's story, a review of the literature, and specific techniques that can be used with the SUD population.

> *There's a crack in everything. That's how the light gets in.*
>
> —*Leonard Cohen*

INTERACTIVE READER COMPONENTS

Case Study 3.1

Your client with SUD has a diagnosis of PTSD. They have:

1. **Reexperienced trauma events:** experience intrusive thoughts, recurrent dreams, and flashbacks reliving trauma events; are emotionally upset during specific time frames associated with specific trauma events; and experience physical/anxiety reactions when reminded of trauma events (e.g., sweaty palms, heart palpitations).

2. **Demonstrated avoidance reactions:** make conscious efforts to avoid thoughts or feelings of trauma events; feel hypervigilant (expect anything bad can happen at any time); tend to isolate; and describe themselves as being robot-like with emotions (i.e., emotionally numb).

3. **Experienced increased arousal:** has periods of trouble sleeping and periods of irritability with occasional anger outbursts; has difficulty concentrating at times and is constantly alert to surrounding events, resulting in being easily startled and "jumpier."

In response to all three areas of PTSD they are experiencing, how would you use the following techniques with them?

- Four-legged stool
- Story and metaphor
- Humor
- Experiential activity and play
- Music

What hesitations would you have in using these techniques with them?

How would you use the guidelines to assist you in assuring them no harm?

With the following exercises, imagine how you might adapt these techniques to your clinical setting (e.g., individual/couple/family/ group) and your SUD population.

Exercise 3.1. Self-Care: Four-Legged Stool

Answer the questions in Box 3C for yourself, and based on your answers, develop a plan for yourself in terms of diet, exercise, sleep, and overall resilience. Then discuss with another person how this might be different for a person with SUD.

Exercise 3.2. Guidelines for Use of Creative Techniques: Uncooked Egg

Take an uncooked egg and carry it with you for a day. Imagine that you are the egg and its hard shell symbolizes your defense mechanisms that protect your vulnerabilities from the harshness of the world. Be aware of what you do with the egg in terms of choices you make on how to protect it. How do you want others to treat your vulnerabilities? Now apply this to a person with SUD. How do you encourage them to be safe as you use these techniques with them?

Exercise 3.3. Guidelines for Use of Creative Techniques: Rubber Band

Take a rubber band and stretch it to its breaking point. Notice the tension you experience as you pull at the band. Now examine how you let the rubber band relax and go back and forth with the band being stretched and relaxing. Again, apply this to a person with SUD you are working with or a person with SUD with whom you plan to work: How do you encourage them to stretch as they try these techniques? What limits do you set with them so they feel safe?

Exercise 3.4. Guidelines for Use of Creative Techniques: Chosen Object

Choose an object that captures how you feel about yourself and then process your thoughts/feelings/reactions to this experience with another person. Now imagine you ask a person with SUD to choose an object that captures how they feel about themselves. As a helping professional, how would you encourage them to explain and process their thoughts and feelings regarding this object with you?

Exercise 3.5. Story and Metaphor

Use the questions in Box 3E that facilitate the person with SUD sharing story of substance use and recovery in a role-play where the other person is in SUD recovery.

Exercise 3.6. Humor

Make a list of humor interventions you use on yourself (e.g., stand-up comedy, comedy movies, comedy television shows, cartoons, jokes). Be specific under each of the interventions in terms of how often you incorporate them in your life and who is with you as you incorporate them. Now discuss with another person how you imagine these interventions would be different for someone in SUD recovery and why.

Exercise 3.7. Experiential Activity and Play

Think about how your culture, as you define it, impacts your play (having fun). Specifically, consider its impact on how play can occur in your life and what is considered appropriate. Now shift it to making a list of questions you would use to explore how culture impacts a person with SUD you are working with or with whom you plan to work.

Exercise 3.8. Music

Have the person with SUD with whom you are working (or imagine the type of person with SUD with whom you plan to work) bring in music that means a lot to them. Then do the following: Ask them to tell you everything they like about the music; examine with them how the music gives them hope; and discuss other kinds of music that would support their SUD recovery.

SUGGESTED READINGS

Readings (Overall)

Stromberg, G., & Merrill, C. (2005). *The harder they fall*. Hazelden.

> This book contains 21 interviews conducted with celebrities or famous individuals that include a congressman, boxer, poet, jockey, rodeo cowboy, and baseball player as well as writers, comedians, musicians, and actors. In each interview, the individual tells their story of becoming addicted to substances and their recovery.

Readings (Humor)

Martin, R. A. (2007). *The psychology of humor: An integrative approach*. Elsevier.

This book, which is both clinically and research based, has 11 chapters. It has an introduction; two chapters on theories of humor; three chapters on the psychology of humor (cognitive, social, developmental); and one chapter each on the psychobiology of humor and laughter; personality approaches to the sense of humor; humor and mental health; humor and physical health, and applications of humor (psychotherapy, education, workplace).

Canha, R. (2020). *Humor and opioid recovery* (Publication No. 13896490) [Doctoral dissertation, University of Maryland–Baltimore]. ProQuest.

This dissertation provides an overview of humor and specifics on its application to opioid use disorder in relation to those individuals in Narcotics Anonymous.

Readings (Music)

Gardstrom, S. C. (2021). *Music as a trigger for substance abuse.* In S. C. Gardstrom & J. Willenbrink-Conte (Eds.), *Music therapy with women with addictions.* Barcelona Publishers.

This chapter on cravings focuses on listening to songs as an intervention technique. The chapter is anchored in research on music and cravings, clinical experience with a residential female population, and provides talking points on a Trigger worksheet the author developed for a 50-minute session focusing on the *what*, *when*, where, and *how* of music listening.

Silverman, M. J. (2022). *Music therapy in mental health for illness management and recovery* (2nd ed.). Oxford University Press.

This 15-chapter book, which is both clinically and research based, covers a wide breadth of content. Specific topics of interest related to SUD include a chapter on SUD that reflects the author's views and an incorporation of addiction in each chapter. Each chapter concludes with a "Main Ideas" section that provides the reader with the main points presented in this densely condensed work.

RESOURCES/WEBSITES

Creativity (Story/Metaphor; Experiential Activity/Play)

International Expressive Arts Therapy Association (IEATA)

https://ieata.org

This international professional organization includes therapists in the expressive arts as well as other professionals (e.g., artists, educators, consultants). IEATA holds conferences, and their website serves as a centralized source of information that encourages growth and transformation both personally and in a community.

Humor

Association for Applied and Therapeutic Humor (AATH)

https://aath.org

This organization holds conferences, and their website contains a research library containing PubMed articles (through the NIH National Library of Medicine, National Center of Biotechnology Information) on studies and application of humor that result in positive change. If one becomes a member of AATH, additional articles are available.

Music

American Music Therapy Association (AMTA)

https://musictherapy.org

This is a nationwide organization that is involved in advocacy, holds conferences, and has journals such as *Musical Therapy Perspectives* and the Journal of Music Therapy that have articles on music therapy in SUD treatment.

Appendices

Appendix 3A: Questions for Exploration of the Four Creative Techniques

QUESTIONS FOR FACILITATING THE PERSON WITH SUD SHARING THEIR STORY OF SUBSTANCE USE AND RECOVERY

1. When was the last time you "sobered up" (e.g., "start time," "sobriety date")?
2. What was the general description of you at the time you reached out for help (e.g., "hit bottom")? What did you look/act like?
3. At that time, did you see yourself as having a substance use problem? If yes, with which substances?
4. What are significant details of your substance use history, especially how/why you started using substances?
5. Who has helped get you into SUD recovery? What did they do? What were they like?
6. What outside supports are important/helpful to your SUD recovery (e.g., AA)?
7. Why are these supports important/helpful to you?

QUESTIONS EXPLORING HUMOR

1. What is humorous to me?
2. How did I experience/express humor as a child? As an adult?
3. What messages did I receive about humor as a child? As an adult?
4. What humor was I allowed as a child? As an adult?
5. How did I see people showing humor when I was a child? As an adult?
6. When is the last time I experienced humor (e.g., laughed)?
7. Who are the people in my life who encourage me to have a sense of humor (e.g., invite laughter in my life)?
8. Where is it safe in my life to incorporate humor (e.g., activities that encourage laughter such as funny movies, comedian performances)?
9. How do I make time to have humor in my life (e.g., spend time with others or take part in activities that encourage laughter)?
10. What are the barriers to me incorporating humor in my life in terms of time, energy, and money? How might I work around these barriers?

QUESTIONS EXPLORING PLAY (I.E., HAVING FUN)

1. What is play (fun) for me with regard to people, places, and activities?
2. How did I play (have fun) as a child? As an adult?
3. What messages did I receive about play (having fun) as a child? As an adult?
4. What play (fun) was I allowed as a child? As an adult?
5. How did I see people playing (having fun) when I was a child? As an adult?
6. When is the last time I played (had fun)?
7. Who are the people in my life who encourage me to play (have fun)?
8. Where is it safe to play (have fun)?
9. How do I make time to play (have fun)?
10. What are the barriers to me playing (having fun) in terms of time, energy, and money? How might I work around these barriers?

GENERAL AND SPECIFIC MUSIC QUESTIONS FOR PEOPLE WITH SUD

General Questions

1. What music are you listening to now? How does it impact you?
2. What music have you listened to when using substances? How did that impact you?
3. What music helps you in your recovery? What does it assist you with (e.g., relaxing)?

Specific Questions

1. What music increases your cravings for substances (i.e., triggers you to use substances)?
2. What music stirs bad memories/experiences for you?
3. What music helps you recover from your negative emotions? What music uplifts your spirit?

Credit

4

PERSONAL DEVELOPMENT IN THE RECOVERY PROCESS

A Developmental, Conceptual Model of Recovery

OBJECTIVES*

1. Use the fourth leg of the self-care framework of the four-legged stool with the person with SUD to explore the spiritual dimension of recovery needed to develop a balanced recovery lifestyle that broadens their perspective and deepens the meaning of their lives.
2. Develop a broader perspective of the SUD recovery community.
3. Understand the "inner war of addiction" (i.e., substances use vs. abstinence) experienced by the person with SUD.

*All objectives are impacted by the incorporation of a theoretical framework that includes a spiritual dimension, such as Jungian psychology.

Overview of the Chapter

This final chapter merges the concepts presented in the previous chapters.

Chapter 1 explored the philosophy of the book and three main concepts:

- the active SUD brain
- the contributing factors to an SUD (e.g., the BioPsychoSocial model)

- the interactive intervention components of the helping relationship, the recovery community, and the approach of "compassionate accountability"

In Chapter 2, the core concepts presented were the collaboration of paraprofessionals and professionals; emotional sobriety; and development of a balanced lifestyle of serenity and hope through recovery communities such as group counseling and/or self-help groups. Chapter 3 presented creative intervention techniques (e.g., story and metaphor; humor; experiential activity and play; and music) through the concepts of:

- the four-legged stool (i.e., balanced lifestyle);
- guidelines for the use of creative techniques; and
- elaboration on the four techniques that assist the person with SUD in developing a balanced recovery lifestyle.

Each of the main concepts of Chapters 1–3 is woven into the tapestry of the developmental, conceptual model of Jungian psychology. This tapestry is the spiritual aspect of the person with SUD—in essence, their psyche (e.g., spirit)—from a Jungian psychology perspective.

First, as in Chapter 3, this chapter opens with the self-care framework of the four-legged stool. However, in this chapter, it is only the fourth leg of the stool that is explored (mind, emotions, spirit). As discussed in Chapter 3, it is this stool leg that is impacted by the creative techniques the helping professional uses with the client with SUD. In this chapter, this stool leg is labeled as the "spiritual aspect" of the person with SUD from a Jungian psychology view. Second, a broader perspective of the SUD recovery community (from the Jungian perspective) is provided in terms of what it offers the person with SUD spiritually in maintaining a balanced recovery. This means the involvement of a "being" larger than oneself, such as the "God of my understanding," nature, group counseling, or self-help groups. Third, the inner war of addiction is presented using Jungian psychology concepts to explain the spiritual struggle within the person with SUD to use substances or to avoid substance use. Understanding this inner war is essential because the helping professional can assist the person with SUD in learning about the aspects of themselves that may lead them to a relapse (e.g., unresolved anger toward their partner that they tend to deny and repress that sparks an urge to use).

Three suggestions for you, the reader, to consider as you read this chapter are:

- *Explore* how you view the spiritual dimension in the lives of human beings, including your own life.
- *Determine* the importance of believing in "something bigger than oneself" for developing balance in one's life.
- *Discover* your views on how a person with SUD can experience a "war of addiction" within themselves.

Exploring one's own spirituality is an aspect of working on the spirituality of a client with SUD. Inclusion of a spiritual practice may assist the health professional in managing stress. The stress management chapter tip in Box 4A contains questions that may help explore one's spiritual practice.

BOX 4A: STRESS MANAGEMENT TIP

Complete the blank.

I feel safe at school/work in these physical spaces (e.g., classroom/office, break room):

_____.

I feel supported at school/work by these people:

_____.

The barriers to my feeling safe/supported in terms of my time, energy, and money are:

_____.

I can work around these barriers by:

_____.

Recovery Story

I try to do the best I can, and I just hope some day they [my children] can look at their father and say, "He tried. He may

not have made it but at least he tried." I am trying through
the Program [Gamblers Anonymous].

—*Anonymous (quoted in Gamblers Anonymous [GA],*
2007, p. 169)

The Story Behind the Statement

A married man with two children, who does not know when
he started compulsively gambling, reflected on his gambling addiction and his recovery through the telling of his
story. He had no history of personal problems. He received
good grades in grammar school and high school, entered
the service, followed by college, where he also graduated
with good grades, and upon graduation from law school,
became an attorney. During college, although he played
cards and went to the racetrack, he did not do so excessively.
His gambling behavior shifted in intensity when he became
an attorney. He described his law practice and himself as
follows: "I started to develop a tremendous law practice,
and I also started to develop a tremendous appetite for
gambling; basically it was casino gambling" (GA, 2007, p.
167). He had a real estate law practice where he was the only
attorney with six secretaries. He reported, "I was making
big money. I could never make from gambling what I could
make out of the practice of law ... but I felt the need, or had
the compulsion, to gamble" (GA, 2007, p. 167). He started
losing more than could be earned. He borrowed money from
banks to cover his gambling debts and would then gamble
with that money. He began to steal money from funds that
did not belong to him, believing that he was only borrowing
money until he got lucky gambling and was able to pay off
the debts. The compulsion to gamble was obsessive: He
lost money, owed money, borrowed money, and took out
five house mortgages. When he found that he could not go
on physically or mentally due to his gambling, he told an
attorney friend and his wife about his gambling. His attorney
friend told him to stop his law practice, warning him, "You
are either going to drive yourself out of your mind or kill
yourself" (GA, 2007, p. 168).

He stopped his practice, and a friend from Gamblers
Anonymous left a note on his door inviting him to talk about

his gambling with him. His wife went with him for the conversation with his friend. The day after their conversation, he attended his first Gamblers Anonymous (GA) meeting. At the meeting, he heard stories that made him realize that he had a gambling problem and he was not the only one who had a gambling problem. He began attending four GA meetings a week, and that continued at the time of his story being written. He stated, "It has been almost three years now, and I haven't gambled on anything—not a lottery ticket, not a chance, not a pinball machine, nothing, not a penny" (GA, 2007, p. 169). In his recovery, he began to feel hope, sleep better, obtain a decent job, become active in the GA fellowship, and speak in high schools and before parole boards about gambling addiction. At the time his story was written, he acknowledged that he would be facing criminal charges for his gambling addiction behaviors: "I know I will have to pay for a criminal act that I committed, and because of GA I am able to face that" (GA, 2007, p. 169). With regard to the ridicule his children and his wife experienced as a result of his gambling addiction, he stated, "The program teaches you to accept the things you cannot change, but don't think it doesn't sometimes hurt" (GA, 2007, p. 169).

Author Personal Reflections

The opening statement for this chapter reflects the gambler's hope to remain abstinent from gambling through participation in GA and to have the respect of his children for changing his life.

In order to talk about SUD recovery, I decided to use the model of AA recovery, which is essentially the same as GA recovery, because of its effectiveness, as discussed in Chapter 2. I also decided to use a theoretical model of Jungian psychology because of its historical impact on AA development. The reader is encouraged to use this integration of a self-help group and a theoretical framework as an example of how, finding something "bigger than oneself" chosen by the person with SUD, in combination with the theoretical framework of the helping professional, can assist in the maintenance of recovery from SUD.

I am taking a risk in this chapter by discussing the fourth leg of the four-legged stool (i.e., mind, emotions, spirit) as the "spiritual dimension" of recovery. This is where the person with SUD who is in recovery begins to rely on something bigger than themselves to remain abstinent. My concern is that a discussion of a spiritual dimension in recovery may be offensive and alienating to the reader. Since we (author, reader) cannot dialogue, my two-fold hope is that you, the reader, will (a) consider my and others' opinions expressed about the spiritual dimension throughout this chapter and (b) decide *if* and *how* you can work with this spiritual perspective within your SUD population.

My decision to include discussion of the spiritual perspective is based on my professional and personal observations of people with SUD. In my observations, I have wondered if the tendency of people with SUD to be obsessive, compulsive, and have perfectionistic standards for their own behavior and that of others is shifted when a spiritual perspective is introduced into recovery. What I have seen has led me to believe that when the person with SUD is focused on the spiritual aspect of recovery, they find a healing, healthy avenue for these tendencies—a sharp contrast to a negative application (e.g., being obsessed with and having compulsive behavior with regard to substance use). These tendencies for reaching the highest spiritual standards have been tempered by AA phrases like "Progress, not perfection," thereby allowing the person with SUD to be "naturally" obsessive, compulsive, and perfectionistic and resulting in those in recovery being some of the finest human beings I have ever met. Those people with SUD who I have witnessed as able to obtain and maintain a balanced recovery have (and use) a supportive recovery community and believe in something bigger than oneself. My hope is that we can stay with each other on this journey of assisting the person with SUD throughout the discussion on the spiritual dimension.

I reverted back to the opening format story section used in the first two chapters (e.g., a quote from a person with SUD followed by a summary of their story). However, the story in this section is about gambling addiction because gambling is the most recent addition to the list of substance use disorders and sometimes is not explored by even the most experienced SUD professionals. Besides inclusion of the story highlighting gambling addiction, it also shows the similarities of gambling with other substances (e.g., alcohol, marijuana) with which the reader may be more familiar. Keep in mind that it is not atypical for someone who has SUD with a substance such as alcohol to also have an SUD with gambling. I also repeat the story to highlight Jungian psychology concepts contained within the story written for Gamblers Anonymous.

In conclusion, this chapter will merge AA and Jungian psychology, resulting in a prototype for the reader. The prototype demonstrates how the spiritual dimension (e.g., AA) combined with the reader's theoretical framework (e.g., Jungian psychology) can assist in the maintenance of recovery of people with SUD.

Self-Care Framework of the Four-Legged Stool

For an explanation of the self-care framework of the four-legged stool, review the opening three paragraphs of the section labeled "Self-Care Framework of the Four-Legged Stool" prior to Box 3C in Chapter 3.

The fourth leg of the stool (mind, emotions, and spirit) is emphasized in this chapter because of its focus on the "spirit" of the person with SUD. Because their focus has been on the use of substances (e.g., "spirit-discouraging"), they need to look at "spirit-encouraging" activities, support networks, and people and incorporate them into their life as much as possible. Early in recovery, the person with SUD needs to make positive changes in caring for themselves spiritually even if they are small changes. This shift will encourage more change and potentially set off a chain reaction of spirit-encouraging changes that can occur throughout the recovery process.

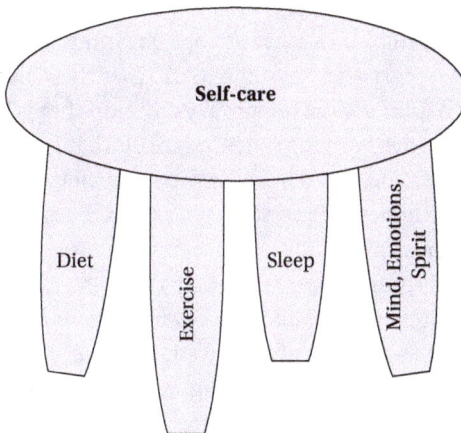

FIGURE 4.1. Self-Care

Educationally, the mental health professional can use the stool to make clients aware of the importance of spiritual self-care in their recovery, advocating that "pretty good" spiritual self-care is enough and self-care does not have to be done perfectly (Miller, 2021). For example, while they may have high standards for how often they attend AA meetings, due to weather conditions, they may not have been able to attend meetings that week as much as they typically attend them. However, if they were able to stay sober, they need reinforcement for the ways they were able to obtain support (e.g., reading more AA literature, contacting their AA sponsor) as well as encouragement to resume their regular meeting attendance ASAP.

In terms of a session check-in, assessment of the fourth leg of the stool (mind, emotions, and spirit), both during the session and in general, reminds the person with SUD that their spiritual well-being is important even during their session with the helping professional. Asking where they are at right now spiritually tells the person with SUD that what they are thinking and feeling and how they are experiencing life is important to the professional. Also, a general check-in on the spiritual component may alert the health professional to issues that need to be addressed in terms of their SUD recovery. For example, they may have had a significant relationship end recently that has resulted in a grief reaction that needs to be processed in the session prior to other concerns because of its impact on their recovery.

Finally, spiritual self-care enhances the possibility of maintaining a balanced recovery lifestyle. The care of one's spirit is as important as the physical needs of diet, exercise, and sleep. It is this leg of the stool that directly impacts a sense of hope, meaning, and fulfillment in recovery that can carry the person with SUD as they "live life on life's terms." While happiness is a temporary emotion that is impossible to maintain all the time, humans can be aware of what is good about their lives, and such awareness can improve their view of the world and their mental health (Rhodes, 2024). Spiritual self-care perpetuates a cycle of increasingly positive self-care strategies in all four legs of the stool that, independently and collectively, help the person with SUD stay in balance in their recovery, resulting in even more self-care strategies.

Although the fourth leg of the stool, spirituality, can positively impact the client's overall well-being, it can also have a history of being "hurtful, damaging or traumatic" (Walsh & Koch, 2023, p. 34). Therefore, the health care professional needs to approach this fourth leg of the self-care stool with an appreciation for individual differences in the SUD population. While understanding a client's spiritual/

religious experiences is important, the health professional needs to be aware that some clients have been traumatized, or at least negatively impacted, by spiritual/religious views as expressed in community with others. Such negative experiences "can thus impact a person's sense of identity, their core beliefs and values, and their perception of safety in the world" (Walsh & Koch, 2023, p. 34). Health professionals need to explore this leg of the stool with caution and sensitivity, always making the therapeutic alliance of safety and care of the client the top priority. The reader is encouraged to read the remainder of the chapter with this caution in mind.

Jungian Psychology Concepts: A Spiritual View

As stated previously in this chapter, the approaches of AA and Jungian psychology are merged, resulting in a prototype for the reader. The purpose of the prototype is to show how an integration of the spiritual dimension (e.g., AA) with the reader's theoretical framework (e.g., Jungian psychology) can assist in SUD recovery. Prior to the presentation of this prototype, a history of the overlap of AA and Jungian psychology is reviewed.

The Story of AA and Jungian Psychology

Miller (2021) and Schoen (2020) provide a summary of the chain of events that led to the development of AA. From its beginning, AA and Jungian psychology were intertwined. The roots of AA are in the psychiatric treatment of Roland, who became sober after alcoholism treatment with the psychiatrist Dr. C. J. Jung in Zurich, Switzerland, in the early 1930s (about 1931). Shortly after 1 year of psychiatric treatment, Roland became sober and then relapsed. He returned to Jung for assistance, and Jung told him that in terms of medical and psychiatric treatment, he was a hopeless case. However, Jung then told him that the hope for him to overcome his drinking problem was to have a conversion experience of a spiritual or religious nature. With that hope in mind, Roland joined the Oxford Group in Europe, an evangelical movement that consisted of nondenominational Christians. The Oxford Group emphasized meditation and prayer as well as following the principles of examining oneself, confessing one's wrongs, practicing restitution for one's wrongs, and dedicating oneself to the service of others. Roland had a conversion experience and returned to New York, joining the Oxford Group there.

Miller (2021) and Schoen (2020) continue in their description of the chain of events. In 1934, Roland, as a part of his Oxford Group service work, met Ebby T., another alcoholic, and introduced him to the Oxford Group. Ebby was a schoolmate of Bill Wilson, who would eventually become one of the cofounders of AA (Bill W.). In November 1934, Ebby visited Bill W. in his home about his drinking problem. He told Bill of his religious experience and introduced him to the Oxford Group. Prior to their visit, Bill had been receiving treatment for his alcoholism by Dr. William Silkworth based on Silkworth's theory that alcoholism was a result of an obsession (compulsion to drink) and an allergic reaction to alcohol resulting in the person becoming worse, insane, or dying. Shortly before Ebby visited Bill, Dr. Silkworth and Bill had experienced the same process that Dr. Jung and Roland had experienced: an admission by Dr. Silkworth of not being able to help Bill recover from his alcoholism and declaration of him as a hopeless case who required commitment. After Ebby visited Bill the first time, Bill entered the hospital under Dr. Silkworth's care and Ebby visited him again in the hospital. Following this second visit, Bill had a conversion experience and subsequently read William Jame's *Varieties of Religious Experience* that described the need of the ego to collapse as a component of the conversion experience. Bill W., then, had a similar experience to Roland.

According to Miller (2021), AA began when Bill, who was a failed Wall Street stockbroker, met Dr. Bob Smith (Dr. Bob, the other cofounder), who was a surgeon in Akron, Ohio. Their meeting was arranged by Mrs. Henrietta Sieberling, an Oxford Group minister, who Bill had contacted after he had failed at a stock takeover bid in Akron. He had contacted her requesting help to meet and talk with another person with alcoholism so he could avoid returning to drinking. She arranged for them (e.g., Bill W. and Dr. Bob) to meet in her home, and 1 month later, after Dr. Bob took his last drink on June 10, 1935, AA was born.

Again, according to Miller (2021), from 1935–1939, approximately 100 members joined AA, and in 1939 the organization obtained its name when its book, *Alcoholics Anonymous*, was published. The book contained a theory of alcoholism, the 12 steps, and stories of people with alcohol use disorder (AUD). Like the 12 steps, the 12 traditions of AA were also based on Oxford Group concepts, and the book that guides the fellowship of AA, *Twelve Steps and Twelve Traditions*, was published in 1946. The AA program consists of both the written 12 steps and the

12 traditions. The AA fellowship, discussed in Chapter 2 of this book, consists of how members interact in community with one another.

The Overlap of AA Concepts and Jungian Psychology Concepts

Schoen (2020) anchors the overlap of the concepts of AA and Jungian psychology in the letters exchanged between Bill W. and Dr. Jung within the span of a week in 1961.

Bill W. wrote a "thank you" letter to Dr. Jung for his significant contribution to the creation of AA. In that letter he told Jung of how his treatment of Roland H. had set off a chain reaction of events that resulted in the creation of AA events of which Dr. Jung was unaware. By pairing the recommendations Jung had made to Roland with the 12 steps of AA, Schoen (2020) outlined how Jung influenced the evolution of AA:

- an admission of powerlessness over alcohol (Step 1);
- the need for something bigger than oneself as the center of consciousness rather than the one's ego (i.e., sense of self) and recognizing that the hope, paradoxically, was in giving up hope of a self-cure **(Step 2)**;
- the surrender of one's ego (e.g., sense of self) to a Higher Power (e.g., Roland finding the Oxford Group) **(Step 3)**; and
- the Oxford Group's emphasis on gratitude, service, and recovery (Steps 4–12) where Step 12 means one alcoholic helps another (e.g., Roland helps Ebby, Ebby helps Bill, Bill helps Dr. Bob).

Essentially, Jung had the message, and Roland was the messenger. One week later, Jung's letter to Bill W. contained Jung's views on alcoholism. From his perspective, he described how Roland wanting spiritual wholeness (i.e., becoming who one is meant to be) and a connection with God was being expressed in his use of alcohol, manifesting as a "low-level thirst for spiritual wholeness, a misplaced worship on the altar of a false idol" (Schoen, 2020, p. 21).

In the letter, Jung stated that the two ways to recovery were religious insight (genuine) and human community that was protective to the individual and consisted of honest, personal relationships (AA; Roy et al., 2022). Jung believed that in order to enter recovery, one *had* to have a spiritual awakening—similar to AA (Schoen, 2020). He also talked about how human community could assist a person in resisting the power of evil (Schoen, 2020).

At the end of his letter, Jung reflected that alcohol, called *spiritus* in Latin, is used for both the highest spiritual/religious experience (healing, grace) as well as the worst poison (evil, darkness). The struggle in addiction, then, is *spiritus contra spiritum* (spirit against spirit; Schoen, 2020). For example, AA (2001) talks about the "hideous Four Horsemen" of "Terror, Bewilderment, Frustration, Despair" (p. 151) that plague a person with active alcohol use disorder and talks about how the fellowship of AA helps protect the person from these fears taking them over.

Schoen (2020) paired the three ways Jung believed people could recover from alcohol use disorder through a connection with God leading to a greater understanding with the first three steps of AA and AA phrases:

- Through "an act of grace" (p. 24): The AA phrase of "hitting bottom" means seeing self and the issue of drinking differently. Step 1 is summarized in the slogan "Don't drink."
- Through "a personal and honest contact with friends" (p. 24): Step 2 is embodied in AA fellowship and summarized in the slogan "Go to meetings."
- Through education of the mind (beyond rational, ego-focused): This corresponds with the AA program of working the 12 steps/having an AA sponsor/reading AA literature. Step 3 is embodied in AA fellowship and summarized in the slogan "Read the Big Book."

This basic formula for recovery through AA is summarized in those three phrases (Miller, 2021):

- "Don't drink": Change one's behavior.
- "Go to meetings": Avoid isolation.
- "Read the Big Book": Read philosophical materials that support recovery.

The tendency to isolate is especially important to address for the person with SUD who, as a result of their substance use, has been increasingly isolated. Research shows that isolation can result in an increased sense of loneliness, while loneliness is diminished with social support (Thompson et al., 2023). Also, social support has been shown to reduce mental health risks (e.g., depression) and possibly help the person experience less stress during stressful events (Thompson et al., 2023). For the person with SUD who is in recovery, then, the social support of attending AA meetings may reduce their sense of loneliness, impact their mental health (e.g., depression), and help them view stressful events as less stressful.

In summary the three phrases above ("Don't drink," "Go to meetings," "Read the Big Book"), reflect Jung's view of recovery from alcohol use disorder. The Jungian psychology perspective on the development of a psychological addiction follows.

Development of a Psychological Addiction from a Jungian Perspective

Jung drew his concepts, his ideas, from history, mythology, anthropology, and religion (Corey, 2017). He developed an analytical, complex psychology (Sharp, 1991). Two core components in Jungian psychology are (a) humans are shaped by both the past and the future and are always changing (e.g., developing, growing, and moving to be more balanced and complete) and (b) the personal shadow (e.g., the dark side of oneself) is a part of being human and needs to be embraced and accepted as a part of oneself but not allowed to dominate the person (Corey, 2017).

In order to understand the development of a psychological addiction from a Jungian perspective, additional Jungian psychology concepts are explained in Box 4B.

BOX 4B: DEFINITIONS OF JUNGIAN CONCEPTS: ARCHETYPE-RELATED

[Note: "archetype" means original model (e.g., prototype)]

Archetypes: the collective unconscious contents that predispose us to human experiences such as birth, love, death, and so on. The *collective unconscious* is the level of the psyche that acts as a "reservoir of latent images" (Hall & Nordby, 1999, p. 39) from the ancestral past, such as a fear of snakes. They are universal-everyone has them. (Hall & Nordby, 1999).

Archetypical image: the form the archetype takes (e.g., dreams, fantasies, etc.).

Archetypical shadow: the demons and Satan-like figures of mythology and religion (Schoen, 2020).

Archetypical shadow/archetypical evil: "an essential ingredient in the psychodynamics of addiction" (Schoen, 2020, p. 45). This is an unintegratable aspect of the psyche (unlike the personal shadow) that occurs when one crosses over into the fifth stage of psychological addiction. It leaves "a perpetual marker, scar, and vulnerability," always making the person susceptible to a relapse back into the addiction (Schoen, 2020, p. 80).

Archetype of the self: the archetype of wholeness, which is the goal of therapy. This *wholeness*, where the unconscious and conscious merge, is also called *individuation*. Individuation is a uniting of opposites that results in becoming who one is meant to be and that also has the key to one's destiny and meaning (Schoen, 2020).

As stated in Box 4B, *archetypes* are the contents of the collective unconscious. Jung believed the *collective unconscious* was the deepest level of the psyche and the hardest to access and that its contents, archetypes, are related to one's family, humanity, and are experienced by everyone (i.e., universal; Corey, 2017). For example, a fear of snakes, from this perspective, comes from the ancestral past and is a fear that passed on through the archetype. The archetyp*ical image* is the form it takes in terms of dreams and fantasies, and dreams are the source of creativity (Corey, 2017). Also, creative activities, such as writing and painting, draw on unconscious forces operating in the individual and are needed to bring the unconscious into consciousness. Additionally, Jung believed dreams help prepare individuals for future experiences in the near future and are a way of balancing opposites (Corey, 2017).

Another term in Box 4B, the *archetypical shadow*, consists of those figures of mythology and religion that serve as images of evil in the unconscious (e.g., the Devil). The *archetype of the self* is where the unconscious and conscious merge (e.g., individuation), and as a result of this merger, there is the wholeness of the person, which is the goal of therapy. In the merger, the *wholeness* of the person consists of who they are meant to be and includes their life destiny and meaning. For example, a person with SUD has not accepted the part of themselves that is angry about how they have been treated unjustly in the world. In denial and repression of this anger, they make the anger a part of their personal shadow. Their personal shadow emerges when they use substances, resulting in a personality change that expresses their anger.

In recovery, with the help of others such as the helping professional, they can learn to recognize how their sense of being treated unjustly in the past has left them with residue anger and learn how to express that anger appropriately. They can learn how to embrace their personal shadow but not let it consume them.

These definitions can be used as a reference for the reader in order to understand the Jungian framework of a psychological addiction. Note that the *archetypical shadow/archetypical evil* mentioned in Box 4B is the part of the psyche that occurs in the process of the fifth stage of the psychological addiction addressed in Table 4.1. Table 4.1 outlines Schoen's (2020) five stages in psychological addiction with the stage term, related Jungian psychology concepts, and application of those concepts to the person with SUD. Whenever possible, this author adapted Shoen's (2020) addiction-related terminology to SUD.

While the table is meant to be self-explanatory in terms of the development of a psychological addiction, the story of gambling addiction at the opening of this chapter is used to assist the reader in understanding the development of SUD. Gambling disorder is the first behavioral addiction to be included in the "Substance-Related and Addictive Disorders" chapter of the American Psychiatric Association's (2013) *Diagnostic and Statistical Manual of Mental Disorders* (5th ed.; *DSM-5*). It was included because of its similarity to how substances activate the brain's reward system (Miller, 2021). Because of its high occurrence with substance use, clinicians are encouraged to screen for both simultaneously (American Psychiatric Association, 2013).

The story of the anonymous person with a gambling addiction is also included to demonstrate the need for both a self-help group (e.g., GA) and a theoretical framework (e.g., Jungian psychology) to obtain and maintain a balanced recovery. The introduction to and reliance on GA is apparent in the story. However, in order to assist the reader in applying Jungian psychology concepts to the story of the person with SUD, the first part of the story is repeated here with statements related to Jungian concepts in bold and Jungian concepts italicized and bolded in brackets.

The first section of the story is paired with the development of a psychological addiction as described in Table 4.1.

A married man with two children, who does not know when he started compulsively gambling, reflected on his gambling addiction and his recovery through the telling of his story. He had no history of personal problems.

TABLE 4.1. The Five Stages in Psychological Addiction (Jungian Psychology)

Stage	Jungian psychology stage term	Main Jungian psychology concepts	Application of Jungian concepts to people with SUD
Stage 1	Ego/persona identification alignment with the false self	**Ego:** sense of "I"; the part of us that is the "air traffic controller" helping us interact with the world as we take in information and make decisions about how we think, feel, act. **Persona:** how we present ourselves; the mask worn that helps us function in the world.	**Weak ego:** result of neglect, abuse, trauma, mental illness, disease, and so on making it hard to deal with inner and outer reality. **Thick/heavy persona:** overidentification with a false self; the image presented to the world.
Stage 2	Personal shadow development	**Personal shadow:** consists of the unacceptable, rejected parts of ourselves; the "psychological garbage can" that becomes increasingly full as we increasingly identify with our persona and have less ego functioning.	**Personal shadow:** The incongruity between one's persona and who one actually is increases; at the same time, the potential for substance abuse increases because more energy is spent denying the shadow's existence through the use of the substance.
Stage 3	Introduction of potentially addictive behavior	**Ego choices (getting help vs. seeking relief):** consists of a struggle between reaching out for assistance (in order to avoid a breakdown) or seeking relief through a coping mechanism that helps reduce tension between the persona and who one actually is.	**Ego choice to seek relief:** belief that help is not needed (denial); sees self as an "exception to the rule," or unlike others who have a problem with the coping mechanism (e.g., substance); potential for SUD is enhanced.
Stage 4	Creation of "Addiction-Shadow-Complex"	**Addiction-Shadow-Complex:** need of the ego to release and express the tension that has resulted from overidentification with the "positively idealized persona" and repression of the "personal shadow."	**Addiction-Shadow-Complex:** occurrence of personality changes when involved with the addictive behavior (SUD related); opportunity for the personal shadow to express itself through the addictive behavior, thereby relieving the tension (e.g., Mr. Hyde supersedes Dr. Jekyll).
Stage 5	Addiction-Shadow-Complex takeover of the psyche	**Addiction-Shadow-Complex:** entire ego, psyche, personality taken over by the Addiction-Shadow-Complex; presence of rationalizations, justifications, and denial with regard to the addictive (SUD-related) behavior.	**Addiction-Shadow-Complex:** continuation of addictive behavior (SUD related) under the Addiction-Shadow-Complex influence; addictive behavior (SUD related) is the #1 priority of the psyche over everything else (e.g., friends; family; etc.); the SUD is all-consuming.

He received good grades in grammar school and high school, entered the service, followed by college, where he also graduated with good grades, and upon graduation from law school, became an attorney. During college, although he played cards and went to the racetrack, he did not do so excessively. **His gambling behavior shifted in intensity when he became an attorney.** [*His personal self began to overidentify with persona of being an attorney.*] He described his law practice and himself as follows: **"I started to develop a tremendous law practice, and I also started to develop a tremendous appetite for gambling; basically it was casino gambling"** (GA, 2007, p. 167). [*His ego/persona aligns with his false self.*] He had a real estate law practice where he was the only attorney with six secretaries. He reported, **"I was making big money. I could never make from gambling what I could make out of the practice of law ... but I felt the need, or had the compulsion, to gamble"** (GA, 2007, p. 167). [*His increased identification with his shadow self resulted in an increased split between his ideal self and his shadow self, resulting in increased tension that fueled the expression of his gambling behavior of his shadow self. The war in addiction begins.*] He started losing more than could be earned. He borrowed money from banks to cover his gambling debts and would then gamble with that money. **He began to steal money from funds that did not belong to him, believing that he was only borrowing money until he got lucky gambling and was able to pay off the debts** [*exception to the rule*]. **The compulsion to gamble was obsessive: He lost money, owed money, borrowed money, and took out five house mortgages.** [*The shadow side had taken over.*] **When he found that he could not go on physically or mentally due to his gambling** [*became physically and psychologically sick*], **he told an attorney friend and his wife about his gambling** [*reached out for help*]. His attorney friend told him to stop his law practice, warning him, **"You are either going to drive yourself out of your mind or kill yourself"** (GA, 2007, p. 168). [*He became psychologically sick.*]

Finally, in his letter to Bill W., Jung suggested there was an archetypal battle of good and evil that takes over the individual in the process of addiction and recovery. During an active addiction, the force of evil is expressed, while in recovery the force of goodness is allowed expression. Schoen (2020) describes this as the inner war of addiction from a Jungian psychology perspective.

Jungian Psychology Concepts: The Inner War of Addiction

In order to understand the inner war of addiction that occurs in both active addiction and recovery from addiction for the person with SUD, additional Jungian psychology concepts are explained in Box 4C.

BOX 4C: DEFINITIONS OF JUNGIAN CONCEPTS RELATED TO ARCHETYPICAL SHADOW/ ARCHETYPICAL EVIL

Archetypical shadow/archetypical evil: The definition of this term is stated in Box 4B.

Humans are drawn to it because of its provision of a sense of power, energy, and freedom as well as having desires met and feeling superhuman (like a god). It creates the illusion of being in control in addition to being special and different from others, thereby making them exempt from the application of typical rules of human behavior. As a part of addiction, it prevents ego insight, control, and adaptation, resulting in an inability to distinguish the truth from lies. This is the unreachable, untouchable aspect of addiction that cannot be touched initially by traditional psychotherapy alone.

Eros: the spiritual power of love, goodness, and light operating on the "principal of love and deep human relationships [that is] protective, healing, and neutralizing of evil" (Schoen, 2020, p. 85). This is the force of light, goodness, and healing.

War of the gods: the divine spiritual warfare linked to the existential question of choosing life or death that is present in both active addiction and addiction recovery (Schoen, 2020).

In this war, in order to be in recovery (e.g., choose life), the person with SUD needs to stay away from the archetypical shadow/arche-

---

typical evil (i.e., not use substances), be in community with others who accept them and hold them accountable for their behavior (e.g., AA), and align themselves with Eros (e.g., experience a power greater than themselves). Alignment with Eros, in combination with a love of community (e.g., AA). is the "weapon" the person with SUD needs in their addiction recovery to win in the spiritual war with the archetypical shadow/archetypical evil. In the recovery process, the person with SUD is humbled by experiencing the archetypical shadow/archetypical evil in their addiction (Step 1 of AA), is open to believing in something bigger than themselves (Step 2 of AA), and is willing to take one step at a time under the guidance of the transcendent force of Eros (Step 3 of AA; Schoen, 2020).

These definitions can be used as a reference for the reader in order to understand the Jungian framework of the inner war of addiction that begins once the person with SUD has "crossed the line" into addiction and is present throughout their recovery.

The definition of the archetypical shadow/archetypical evil (e.g., the Devil) previously mentioned in Box 4B is expanded on in Box 4C. It is a force of darkness, evil, and death that expresses itself in the person with SUD during their *active use*. While this can be thought of as a dramatic description, often those in the presence of the person with SUD in active addiction will tell stories of unbelievable behaviors toward others of the person with SUD while under the influence of the substance. For example, the person with SUD who typically is loving toward their children is extremely physically violent toward them when under the influence of the substance. This is the force that is allowed "entry" into the behavior of the active addiction of the person with SUD and is the "opening" that occurs in the process of the fifth stage of the psychological addiction addressed in Table 4.1.

Eros, another definition in Box 4C, is the opposing force that is the force of light, goodness, and healing that is expressed in the thoughts, behaviors, and motives of the person with SUD who is in recovery.

The final definition in Box 4C, the *war of the gods*, is the spiritual warfare within the person with SUD that is present in both active addiction and recovery. This spiritual warfare is present in both active addiction and recovery because, as with any chronic disease (e.g., cancer), the disease may cease being active (i.e., go into remission) as a result of the recovery behaviors of the person with SUD in their recovery healing process. However, the person with SUD needs to be watchful of signs of its reactivation (potential relapse) throughout their recovery as they experience the inner war of addiction.

Table 4.2 describes the healing process in recovery by depicting where the 12 steps of AA are divided into Sections A, B, and C from a Jungian psychology perspective and how they correspond with the six stages of the healing process and recovery (Schoen, 2020). These three areas merge the terms (that were used in Table 4.1) with the 12 steps of AA, demonstrating the overlap between the 12 steps of AA and Jungian psychology concepts.

To assist the reader in understanding the overlap of the two perspectives, a description of the AA 12 Step Program's steps and philosophy is included here (Table 4.3) to assist the reader in understanding how the colloquial language of AA, discussed in Chapter 2, is expanded on in terms of its application to the steps and the philosophy of AA.

While the table is self-explanatory, a couple of items need to be noted. First, AA and Jungian psychology place Step 10 in different categories, as noted in Tables 4.2 and 4.3. AA groups this step, which involves taking a personal inventory of oneself on a continual basis, with two other maintenance steps (Steps 11 and 12). This AA grouping emphasizes the importance of the person with SUD embracing their personal shadow as a part of maintenance of recovery balance. However, from a Jungian psychology framework, Step 10 is grouped with the action steps (Steps 4–9), emphasizing the importance of personal shadow work as a part of the action stage of recovery.

Second, Table 4.3 notes that the words that stress community ("we," "our," "us") are absent in Steps 6 and 9, which address a willingness to let a Higher Power remove one's defects of character and making direct amends to others, respectively.

Table 4.4 compares the 12 steps of AA with Jungian concepts and perspectives to assist the reader in seeing the complimentary overlap of the two perspectives of recovery. Again, whenever possible, this author adapted Schoen's (2020) addiction-related terminology to SUD.

TABLE 4.2. The Healing Process of Recovery Through the Twelve Steps of Alcoholics Anonymous

THE TWELVE STEPS

A
1. We admitted we were powerless over alcohol—that our lives had become unmanageable.
2. Came to believe that a Power greater than ourselves could restore us to sanity.
3. Made a decision to turn our will and our lives over to the care of God as we understood Him.

B
4. Made a searching and fearless moral inventory of ourselves.
5. Admitted to God, to ourselves, and to another human being the exact nature of our wrongs.
6. Were entirely ready to have God remove all these defects of character.
7. Humbly asked Him to remove our shortcomings.
8. Made a list of all persons we had harmed, and became willing to make amends to them all.
9. Made direct amends to such people wherever possible, except when to do so would injure them or others.
10. Continued to take personal inventory, and when we were wrong promptly admitted it.

C
11. Sought through prayer and meditation to improve our conscious contact with God as we understood Him, praying only for knowledge of His will for us and the power to carry that out.
12. Having had a spiritual awakening as the result of these steps, we tried to carry this message to alcoholics, and to practice these principles in all our affairs.

THE HEALING PROCESS AND RECOVERY STAGES

A
1. Ego disidentifies with the persona/false self
2. Recognition of the ego under the addiction-shadow complex's control
3. Relativizing of the ego as the center of the psyche

B
4. Confronting and integrating the personal shadow

C
5. Ongoing maintenance of the ego–self axis
6. Living in service with the Self

Adapted from Schoen (2020)

TABLE 4.3   AA 12 Step Program: Steps and Philosophy for Person with SUD

The 12 Steps of AA	*AA Philosophy*
(Colloquial language of steps varies among individuals, groups, etc.)	**Use slogans associated with a 12-step program "way of living":** *"One day at a time."* *"First things first."* *"Easy does it."* *"Let go and let God."* *"Act as if."* **Remember, "God" is defined by an individual's conception of God** **(God = Higher Power)**
Steps 1–3 **"Admission of powerlessness"** **and "Letting go to a God (Higher Power)" steps**	**Be aware of words ("we," "our, "us") in Steps 1–3 that stress community.** <u>**Use 12-step phrases to understand Steps 1–3:**</u> **Step 1:** "I can't" (e.g., "hitting bottom"). **Step 2:** "He can." ("He" = God = Higher Power). **Step 3:** "I think I'll let Him." ("Him" = God = Higher Power).
Steps 4–10* **Action steps** ***AA (in contrast to Jungian psychology) includes Step 10 with the maintenance steps**	**Be aware of words in the steps ("we," "our," "us") that stress community** **(except in Steps 6 and 9).** **Step 4:** -Start inventory anchored in the seven deadly sins (AA, 1991): pride, greed, lust, anger, gluttony, envy, and sloth. -Take one's own inventory, not the inventories of others.
	Step 5: -Examine both the positive and the negative aspects of oneself. -Use "ruthless self-honesty" (Schoen, 2020, p. 113). -Confess all one's secrets to a good listener who has compassion. -"[In so doing], you have swallowed and digested some big chunks of truth about yourself" (AA, 2001, p. 71). **Step 6:** -Be willing to have God (Higher Power) remove personal defects of character.

	Step 7: -Ask God (Higher Power) to remove these personal defects of character (shortcomings). **Step 8:** -Make a list of those who have been harmed by one's substance use and have a willingness to make amends for actions during substance use (e.g., practically and/or metaphorically "pay back debts"). -Define the word "amend" to mean making "a mend" in past and current relationships. -Place one's self at the top of the amend list because in every situation where harm was done to others, one's self was present and thereby experienced harm also. **Step 9:** -Make direct amends to those individuals harmed. **Step 10:*** -Self-examine, ongoingly, one's thoughts, behaviors, and motives with a prompt willingness to admit wrongdoing. *AA (in contrast to Jungian psychology) includes Step 10 with the maintenance steps.
*Steps 11–12** Maintenance steps *AA (in contrast to Jungian psychology) includes Step 10 with the maintenance steps	**Be aware of words in the steps ("we," "our," "us") that stress community.** **Step 11:** -Use prayer and meditation to improve conscious contact with God (Higher Power). -The words "prayer," "meditation," and "God" are open to individual interpretation. **Step 12:** -After working through the other 11 steps, one has a spiritual awakening that results in sharing what they have learned in 12-step recovery with others who struggle with substance use. They also need to live the 12-step program principles in their daily life. Paradoxically, one's recovery program is strengthened through the process of "giving it away" to others.

(AA, 1991, 2001; Miller, 2021; Schoen, 2020)

TABLE 4.4   Comparison of AA Steps and Jungian Concepts and Perspective

The 12 steps of AA	Jungian concepts involved in healing process of Recovery (Schoen, 2020)	Jungian perspective: healing process and recovery stages (Schoen, 2020)
[Note: Colloquial language of steps varies among individuals, groups, etc.]		(These six stages of healing and recovery are in reverse order of the five stages listed in Table 4.1 because *what occurred last in the development of the psychological addiction needs to be addressed first in the healing and recovery process.*)
		__Group A on Table 4.1 Chart__
Steps 1–3 **Admission of powerlessness and letting go to a Higher Power steps**	*Ego deflation* -Ego recognition of the addiction-shadow complex -Ego disidentification with false self -Ego surrender to a higher spiritual power	Stage 1: The ego disidentifies with the persona/false self. Stage 2: Recognition of the ego under addiction-shadow complex control occurs. Stage 3: The ego is revitalized as the center of the psyche. __Goal:__ Shift consciousness to the perspective of not having the answers, not being able to figure the addiction out, and not being able to control the addiction.
		__Group B on Table 4.1 Chart__
Steps 4–10* **Action steps** *AA (in contrast to Jungian psychology) includes Step 10 with the maintenance steps.	*Ego insight* -Personal shadow work	Stage 4: Confronting and integrating the *personal shadow* occurs. __Goal:__ Make self a better person by seeing self more realistically and objectively resulting in humility; in other words, "eat one's shadow" (Schoen, 2020, p. 117). __Group C on Table 4.1 Chart__
Steps 11–12* **Maintenance steps** *AA (in contrast to Jungian psychology) includes Step 10 with the maintenance steps.	*Strong, vital ego and self relationship is maintained.* *Individuation as expressed in service*	Stage 5: Ongoing maintenance of the *ego–self* axis occurs. __Goal:__ Become more conscious of God (Higher Power). Stage 6: *Living in service* with the self occurs. __Goal:__ Become more responsible to self, others, and the world as a result of being more conscious of God (Higher Power).

To assist the reader in understanding the inner war of addiction, the second section of the story of the anonymous person with a gambling addiction is provided here. The story reflects how the person had to make a choice to reach out to other human beings and a Higher Power in order to enter into and remain in recovery. Statements related to Jungian concepts are in bold, and Jungian concepts are bolded and italicized in brackets throughout the story:

> He stopped his practice, and a friend from Gamblers Anonymous left a note on his door inviting him to talk about his gambling with him. **His wife went with him for the conversation with his friend. The day after their conversation, he attended his first Gamblers Anonymous (GA) meeting** [*reached out for help*]. At the meeting, he heard stories that made him realize that he had a gambling problem and he was not the only one who had a gambling problem. He began attending four GA meetings a week, and that continued at the time of his story being written. **He stated: "It has been almost three years now, and I haven't gambled on anything—not a lottery ticket, not a chance, not a pinball machine, nothing, not a penny" (GA, 2007, p. 169)** [*reliance on a power—GA— bigger than self*]. In his recovery, he began to feel hope, sleep better, obtain a decent job, become active in the GA fellowship, and speak in high schools and before parole boards about gambling addiction. At the time his story was written, he acknowledged that he would be facing criminal charges for his gambling addiction behaviors: "I know I will have to pay for a criminal act that I committed, and because of GA I am able to face that" (GA, 2007, p. 169). With regard to the ridicule his children and his wife experienced as a result of his gambling addiction, he stated: "The program teaches you to accept the things you cannot change, but don't think it doesn't sometimes hurt" (GA, 2007, p. 169).

The second section of the story demonstrates the need for the person with SUD to both attend a self-help group (e.g., GA) and have a theoretical framework (e.g., Jungian psychology) to obtain and maintain a balanced recovery. The introduction to and reliance on GA is apparent in the story.

Jungian Psychology Dream Interventions with the Person with SUD

The reader, unless trained in Jungian dream analysis, may be concerned about "analyzing" the dreams of a person with SUD who is in recovery because they view themselves as practicing outside their area of competence. However, this author encourages the helping professional to process the reactions of the person with SUD to having a "using dream" (i.e., a dream where they are either using a substance or are tempted to do so) during their recovery for three reasons. First, the person with SUD may have a strong reaction to their dream and not have a safe place to admit to having one. Second, the dream(s) may hold important clinical information regarding "diagnosis, prognosis, and treatment of addiction" (Schoen, 2020, p. 127). Third, dreams can help the person with SUD in recovery heal and acknowledge their limits (Schoen, 2020). In summary, using dreams needs to be taken seriously because they can tell helping professionals where the client with SUD is in terms of their commitment to recovery, warn of relapse, and encourage changes/interventions that need to be made in the client's recovery (Schoen, 2020).

The key in this analysis of a using dream may be in a careful, thoughtful approach using motivational interviewing (MI) strategies that draw out the focus of the "dream story" of the client with SUD. This approach needs to be used within the therapeutic alliance, an, rather than following a formula for analysis, the dream needs to be processed with consideration of the idiosyncratic features of the person with SUD and their life circumstances (Schoen, 2020). Some questions that can be used in the processing of a using dream with client with SUD in recovery include:

- What is your addiction trying to tell you in this dream?
- What might we learn about your recovery from this dream?
- What struggle inside of you about recovery is this dream communicating with you (e.g., staying sober vs. returning to using)?

Schoen's (2020) presentation on Jungian analysis of dreams is based on (a) a 2-year self-report survey given to people with SUD and alcohol use disorder (AUD) in a drug treatment facility from 1990 through 1991 (104 respondents); (b) interviews/discussions with individuals and groups with sobriety ranges of 1 day to 40 years; and (c) tracking the dreams of people with SUD and AUD in recovery in his Jungian analysis practice.

He found the following tendencies for people with SUD and AUD:

- reduced recall of their dreams compared to the general population
- blocked dreams or diminished recall of dream details

As stated previously, Corey (2017) and Schoen (2020) summarized the Jungian psychology of the view of dreams:

- The image of the archetype is in the form it takes in a dream.
- Creative activities (e.g., writing, painting) draw from the unconscious forces in the individual and can be used to bring the unconscious into consciousness.
  Dreams help individuals prepare for near-future life experiences as well as balance opposites within the psyche.

Box 4D contains Jungian dream definitions to assist the reader in the processing of using dreams with a person with SUD who is in recovery.

BOX 4D: JUNGIAN DREAM DEFINITIONS (SCHOEN, 2020)

Using dream: The person with SUD is either using a substance or is tempted to use a substance in a dream.

Dream ego: "It is what we hear, see, feel, smell, say, think, touch, imagine, and do in the dream itself. It is the character or aspect of the dream we refer to as 'I' when we tell the story of the dream" (Schoen, 2020, p. 130)

Waking ego: This "is what we normally identify as the 'I' in our everyday waking life, our reactions and experiences and perceptions of things, etc." (Schoen, 2020, p. 130).

Dream ego reaction*: This is the reaction of the dream ego to the substance use in the dream. These reactions vary in terms of and depend on length of sobriety; attitude toward sobriety/recovery; and active involvement in recovery (e.g., community, 12-step program, reading literature, etc.).

Waking ego reaction*: This is the reaction of the waking ego to the substance use in the dream. These reactions vary in terms of and depend on length of sobriety; attitude toward sobriety/recovery; and active involvement in recovery (e.g., community, 12-step program, reading literature, etc.).

*Recommendation:
Compare and contrast the dream ego reaction and the waking ego reaction.

Box 4D needs to be used in conjunction with Table 4.5 that outlines dream ego reactions and waking dream reactions to the dream of a client with SUD. Both dream ego and waking ego reactions to the dream operate on a Likert scale continuum, with *feels great to use* at one end of the continuum and at the other end of the continuum. The intensity of these reactions on a continuum needed to be processed with the person with SUD. The comparison of the dream ego and waking ego reactions needs to occur in the dialogue with the person with SUD about their type of dream: "feels great" using dream; "feels awful" using dream; "somewhere-in-between" using dream.

It can be easy to become lost in the Jungian terminology of dreams. At the risk of being overly simplistic, when looking at Table 4.5, the feels great using dream can be thought of metaphorically as two people in agreement with one another about a behavior. The feels awful using dream can be viewed as two people disagreeing with one another's perspective about a behavior. The somewhere-in-between using dream captures the fluctuation between two individuals who vary in their perspective about a behavior. These metaphors summarize the war of addiction in the person with SUD as they are in their healing, their process of recovery.

There are two main takeaways from this section:

- Analysis of using dreams is important for people with SUD because of the rich amount of clinical information that can be obtained.
- The helping professional can analyze dreams if the dream processing is approached carefully and thoughtfully, always focusing on the reactions of the person with SUD to the dream and taking into consideration who they are and their life circumstances in order to make appropriate relapse prevention interventions.

TABLE 4.5 Using Dream Reactions

	"Feels great" using dream reactions		
Dream ego reaction	Waking ego reaction	Relapse warnings	Changes/interventions needed in supports/recovery process
"Feels great" -Pleasure/enjoyment with using/being tempted by the substance in the dream -Absence of guilt/anxiety/sense of failure/remorse	"Feels great" -Pleasure/enjoyment with using/being tempted by the substance in the dream -Absence of guilt/anxiety/sense of failure/remorse	**Under 3 years sobriety (early recovery):** Person with SUD is under the influence of the addiction-shadow complex: 1–3 -Has not worked AA's Steps 1–3 -Has not "hit bottom" -Is not invested in recovery **After 3 years recovery:** -Person with SUD is being influenced by the addiction-shadow complex.	**STOP** Look at the support system and the recovery program to assess necessary revisions needed to prevent relapse.

		"Feels awful" using dream reactions		
Dream ego reaction	**Waking ego reaction**	**Relapse warnings**		**Changes/interventions needed in supports/recovery process**
"Feels awful"	**"Feels awful"**	**Later in sobriety (recovery) (e.g., when the person is strongly committed to the AA program):**		CAUTION
-Upset, uneasy, ambivalent feelings in response to using/ being tempted by the substance in the dream	-Wonder why the dream occurred and what it means in terms of recovery	-Dream indicates a commitment to recovery that is greater than the commitment to addiction.		Reminders to the person with SUD that they: -are still addicted -need to avoid overconfidence -need to be aware of vulnerability (e.g., excessive stress; poor self-care) and reduce stress and reprioritize
-Presence of feelings of "fear, failure, guilt, shame, disappointment, anxiety and remorse" (Schoen, 2020, p. 141)	**"Feels awful"/ "Feels relief"**	-Dream indicates the archetypal shadow/archetypal evil aspect of the addiction-shadow complex is neutralized, allowing the "war" to be fought at the human, not archetypal, level because the ego is healthier as a result of recovery.		-Urgently explore the unusual split because it could be an "exceptional circumstance physically, psychologically, socially, or spiritually" (e.g., grief, depression, existential crisis, etc.; (Schoen, 2020, p. 143).
	-Initially upset because they believe they relapsed and then feel relief that they are still sober			
"Feels awful"/ "Feels great" -Sometimes mixed pleasure	-Wonder why the dream occurred and what it means in terms of recovery			

Dream ego reaction	Waking ego reaction	**"Somewhere-in-between" using dream reactions**	
		Relapse warnings	Changes/interventions needed in supports/recovery process
Most convoluted of the reactions:			
"There is truly a mixture, a combination of varying reactions to both the dream ego in the using dream as well as the waking ego afterwards, with a variety of different reactions coming at different times from the same person" (Schoen, 2020, p. 144).		-Sometimes the person with SUD is committed to recovery. -Sometimes the person with SUD is ambivalent about recovery.	Sort the various reactions out with the person to determine their issues related to their recovery and then decide on appropriate interventions that fit the person and their unique life circumstances.

Adapted from Schoen (2020)

Time Markers of Relapse Vulnerability in Recovery

Relapse prevention interventions during the recovery of a person with SUD hinge on the length of recovery, as noted in Table 4.5 related to Jungian psychology dream interpretation. First, however, in order to understand appropriate and timely relapse prevention strategies, such as in Jungian psychology dream analysis, the term "recovery" needs to be defined and a framework of recovery needs to be provided in terms of recovery time frames.

The Betty Ford Institute Consensus Panel (2007), which consisted of researchers, treatment providers, recovery advocates, and policymakers, met to develop an initial definition of recovery for the purpose of enhanced communication, research, and understanding by the public. The panel's definition of *recovery* was "a voluntarily maintained lifestyle composed characterized by sobriety, personal health and citizenship" (Betty Ford Institute Consensus Panel, 2007, p. 221). At this meeting, "stable recovery" was determined to be established at 5 years.

Later, Martinelli et al. (2020) described recovery as a gradual, long-term process related to life domains that consists of housing, crime, work/education, and substance use. They provided a recovery framework of "early recovery" as less than 1 year; "sustained recovery" as 1–5 years, and "stable recovery" as 5 years and beyond; the latter interval is similar to the Betty Ford Institute Consensus Panel's (2007) determination.

What is known about relapse vulnerability (e.g., time markers of vulnerability) at different recovery stages in terms of interventions? Because most relapses happen in the first few months (approximately 3 months) after treatment, the intervention of aftercare needs to be more intense during that time (Nordfjaern, 2011). This indicates that the person with SUD is extremely vulnerable to relapse in the first 3 months of recovery. Yet, little is known about why recovery occurs and the mechanisms and mediators that are core to addiction recovery (Vanderplasschen & Best, 2021). That means that there is little known about what needs to be present for recovery to occur as well as be maintained.

In light of all that is unknown in research, the author, through consultations with AA sponsors and over 40 years of personal and professional observations of friends and clients with SUD , has developed time markers of vulnerability in recovery as well as behaviors indicating possible relapse and related intervention strategies. Some of these coincide with the AA system of giving out medallion or "chips" to mark certain periods of time in recovery. "Sometimes a beginner medallion or a 'white chip' is given to someone new or returning to recovery. Typically, they are given at intervals of 1, 3, 6, 9, 12, and 18 months and then yearly" (Miller, 2021, p. 239). The time markers of relapse vulnerability in recovery and behaviors indicating possible relapse and related intervention strategies are listed in Box 4E.

BOX 4E: TIME MARKERS OF RELAPSE VULNERABILITY IN RECOVERY*: RELAPSE-ENCOURAGING BEHAVIORS AND INTERVENTION STRATEGIES

*Caution: These time frames are not research-based but are based on the personal observations of AA sponsors and personal/professional observations of the author. The time frames also need to be "held loosely" because not all people with SUD will experience any or all of these times of relapse vulnerability.

Time Markers

Time markers that coincide with the AA medallion ("chip") system:

1, 3, 6, 9, 12 (1 year), and 18 months, then yearly beginning at 2 years.

Additional observed year markers of relapse vulnerability:

5 years, 7 years, 10- to 15-year time frame (10- to 15-year time frame vulnerability possibly related to a deep, old, unresolved issue of trauma, grief, etc.).

Behaviors Indicating Possible Relapse

1. Use of defenses of denial/projection/rationalization when confronted on inappropriate behavior toward others.
2. Tendency to intellectualize and cut off from emotions.
3. Dichotomous (right/wrong) thinking.
4. Refusal to ask for help with life struggles/emotions (e.g., "I've got recovery down pat and don't need anyone's help").
5. Reduction or elimination of support from others (e.g., not attending AA meetings/not calling AA sponsor as often or not at all).
6. "Talking the talk but not walking the walk" in terms of the AA program.

Relapse-Prevention Behavioral Interventions

■ In a caring, supportive, calm, and firm manner confront the SUD person on the behaviors of Items 1–4 above.
■ Regarding Item 5, encourage resumption of AA activities, which will shift Item 6 to "walking the walk."

Figure 4.2 links AA's time markers of relapse vulnerability with the "war of the gods in addiction" (Schoen, 2020). In the war of the gods, as stated previously in Box 4C:

> In order to be in recovery (e.g., choose life), the addict needs to stay away from the archetypical shadow/archetypical evil (e.g., not use), be in community with others who accept them and hold them accountable for their behavior (e.g., AA), and align themselves with Eros (e.g., experience a power greater than themselves). Alignment with Eros, in combination with a love of community (e.g., AA), is the antidote the addict needs in their addiction recovery to win in the spiritual war with the archetypical shadow/archetypical evil. In the recovery process, the addict is humbled by experiencing the archetypical shadow/archetypical evil in their addiction (Step 1 of AA), is open to believing in something bigger than themselves (Step 2 of AA), and is willing to take one step at a time under the guidance of the transcendent force of Eros (Step 3 of AA). (Schoen, 2020)

This war is also reflected in the following tables in this chapter:

■ Table 4.2 that presents the healing process of recovery stages (Groups A, B, C in Table 4.1)

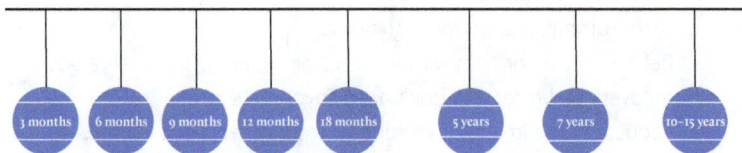

FIGURE 4.2   AA Time Markers of Relapse Vulnerability linked to *The War of the Gods: Life or Death Choice* (Schoen, 2020)

- Table 4.3 in terms of working the 12 steps of AA
- Table 4.4 with the six stages of the healing process and recovery (Schoen, 2020)

In Table 4.4, the choice of life is clearly demonstrated in the goals of the six stages of the healing process and recovery (Schoen, 2020). In Stages 1–3 (Group A in Table 4.1), the goal is a shift in consciousness to the perspective of not having the answers, not being able to figure the addiction out, and not being able to control the addiction. In Stage 4 (Group B in Table 4.1), the goal is to make oneself a better person by seeing oneself more realistically and objectively, resulting in humility. In Stages 5 and 6 (Group C in Table 4.1), the goal is to become more responsible to oneself, others, and the world (Stage 6) as a result of being more conscious of God/Higher Power (Stage 5).

At times, especially during a time of vulnerability for the person with SUD, a part of relapse prevention in recovery involves letting go of significant people in their life. During the recovery of the person with SUD, these individuals have shown a tendency to

- refuse to self-examine;
- refuse to dialogue about the interpersonal struggle(s) between themselves and the person with SUD;
- demonstrate an unwillingness to change their hurtful behavior toward the person with SUD;
- be closed to any feedback they perceive as critical or negative; and
- use "Teflon defenses" of denial and projection with the person with SUD (e.g., "Our problems are all your fault").

The person with SUD who is in recovery needs to be aware that in letting go of this significant person, they may hear verbally stated or implied shaming and/or guilting strategies stemming from anger, such as "I cared for you when no one else would in your active substance use and *now*, in your recovery, you treat me like *this*." This is when, once again, the recovery community can be supportive of the person with SUD as they make this change in their recovery.

A sample of this "spiritual letting go" process is provided in Box 4F, which contains a form letter that may or may not be sent to the person whom they loved and who loved them up until this point in their recovery.

> ## BOX 4F: "SPIRITUAL LETTING GO" FORM LETTER
>
> Dear _____,
>
> I cannot remain on this life journey with you because you will probably continue to hurt me as you struggle with your fears. Therefore,
>
> - I am choosing life.
> - I am choosing to be with people who will both love me and show me loving and respectful behavior.
> - I am choosing to protect my heart in order to stay sober.
> - I am choosing to protect my spirit in order to stay sober.
>
> I wish you the very best on your life journey as you continue on it without me.
>
> Sincerely,
>
> _____ (my name)

SUMMARY

In summary, three main areas were reviewed in this chapter. First, the four-legged stool self-care framework that encourages a balanced recovery lifestyle was explored in terms of the fourth leg of spirituality (mind, emotions, spirit). The importance of incorporating this component in establishing and maintaining the recovery of the person with SUD was stressed. Second, the inclusion of the integration of a theoretical model (e.g., Jungian psychology) and an SUD recovery community (e.g., AA) was explored. This integration provided a more panoramic view of the SUD recovery and the SUD recovery community. Third, the concept of "the inner war in addiction" that elaborated on the importance of the person with SUD embracing their "shadow self" in order to establish and maintain their SUD recovery was introduced. This included the area of using dream analysis that can be beneficial to the person with SUD.

KEY POINTS

1. The fourth leg of the four-legged stool self-care framework was expanded on in this chapter because of its importance in the development of a balanced recovery lifestyle. This spiritual aspect of the person is necessary to broadening the perspective of the person with SUD and deepening their life meaning. Without it, their vulnerability to relapse is increased.

2. A broader perspective of the SUD recovery community that includes a spiritual view (e.g., Jungian psychology) was presented. This perspective increases the probability of the maintenance of SUD recovery.

3. Through understanding the "inner war in addiction" of the person with SUD (e.g., substances use vs. abstinence), the helping professional can assist the person with SUD in embracing their "shadow self" rather than repressing it. The embracing of the shadow self means that the person with SUD has an enhanced opportunity to stay sober because they are acknowledging and examining their flaws and issues rather than denying them, which could take them back to using substances.

> *When you come to the edge of all that you know, you must believe in one of two things: There will be earth upon which to stand, or you will be given wings.*
>
> *—Author unknown*

INTERACTIVE READER COMPONENTS

Case Study 4.1

Your client with SUD, who is in Stage 5 psychological addiction ("The Addiction-Shadow Complex Takeover of the Psyche"; Table 4.1), reports to you that they have recently had a "using dream." You need to explore the dream with them because it has been upsetting to them. They have over 3 years of sobriety and are very committed to AA (e.g., attending meetings, working the steps, calling their sponsor). They felt awful during the dream about using the substance and felt awful about it when they woke up. They are concerned about what this dream means and do not feel safe talking with anyone else about their dream. Be aware of what concerns you would have about discussing their dream with them and how you would work with those concerns. Use the following boxes and tables to assist you in talking with the client about their dream.

1. **Box 4D:** How would you use the terms in this box to help them understand their dream?
2. **Table 4.5:**
   o Based on their description of their reactions to the dream, how would you compare and contrast the dream ego reaction and the waking ego reaction in a language they would understand?
   o What feelings would you expect them to have in reaction to the dream? How would you process those feelings with them?
   o Which changes/intervention cautions would you talk with them about?

With the following exercises, imagine how you might adapt these concepts/techniques to your clinical setting (e.g., individual/couple/family/group) and your SUD population. Use the questions listed as a guide for your discussion on adaptation of the concepts/techniques with a colleague/supervisor/mentor.

Exercise 4.1. Box 4B: Definitions of Jungian Concepts: Archetype-Related

How would you use the term "archetype of wholeness" to help your client with SUD understand how you are trying to assist them as a helping professional?

Exercise 4.2. Box 4C: Definitions of Jungian Concepts Related to Archetypical Shadow/ Archetypical Evil

How would you use these definitions to explain "the inner war of addiction" in your client with SUD?

Exercise 4.3. Table 4.1: The Five Stages in Psychological Addiction

How would you explain Stage 5 ("The Addiction-Shadow Complex Takeover of the Psyche") to your client in terms of their rationalizations, justifications, and denial about their substance use?

Exercise 4.4. Table 4.2: The Healing Process of Recovery Through the 12 Steps of AA

How would you use this table to assist your client with SUD in understanding Sections A, B, and C as they relate to the 12 steps?

How would you explain Section B, "Confronting and integrating the personal shadow," in terms of Steps 4–10?

Exercise 4.5. Table 4.3: AA 12-Step Program— Steps and Philosophy for People with SUD

How would you use the AA breakdown of the steps (first three steps, action steps, maintenance steps) to help them understand the AA model of recovery?

Exercise 4.6. Table 4.4: Comparison of AA Steps and Jungian Concepts and Perspective

How would you use the six stages of healing and recovery to help your client understand the thre goals of recovery (i.e., Stages 1–3; Stage 4; Stages 5–6)?

SUGGESTED READINGS

Readings (Overall)

Galvani, S., G., Roy, A., & Clayson, A. (Ed.) (2022). *Long-term recovery from substance use: European perspectives*. Policy Press.

> This edited book is divided into three parts that contain chapters written by different authors. Part I, "Critical Explorations of Long-Term Recovery," contains five chapters (the first chapter is written by the editors); Part II, "Intimate Relationship, Trauma and Long-Term Recovery," has four chapters containing stories of people with SUD internationally; and Part III, "diversity Across the Lifespan in Long-Term Recovery," has five chapters. (Four of them focus on specific populations, while the last chapter, on conclusions, is written by the editors.)

Readings (Gambling)

Gamblers Anonymous. (2007). *Gamblers Anonymous.*

> This book is considered the main text of Gamblers Anonymous and has eight chapters that cover main areas of the disorder. It also has an epilogue, five appendices, and a bibliography. Chapter 8 consists of stories of individuals who have the disorder.

Gamblers Anonymous. (1989). *Gamblers Anonymous* (5th ed.).

> This book has nine chapters that describe the organization of Gamblers Anonymous and a final chapter that is an epilogue.

Readings (Jungian Psychology)

Hall, C. S., & Nordby, V. J. (1999). *A primer of Jungian psychology.* Meridian.

> This book consists of seven chapters. The first chapter focuses on Jung, the next five chapters provide an overview of Jungian psychology (personality structure, personality dynamics, personality development, psychological types, symbols and dreams), and the seventh chapter is a summary of Jung's place in psychology.

Jung, C. J. (Ed.). (1964). *Man and his symbols: Approaching the unconscious.* Dell.

> The introduction of this book, the last work written by Jung before his death, was written by the coordinating editor, John Freeman. The five sections of the book are titled "Approaching the Unconscious" (written by Jung); "Ancient Myths and Modern Man"; "The Process of Individuation"; "Symbolism in the Visual Arts"; and "Symbols in an Individual Analysis." It has a conclusion that focuses on science and the unconscious.

Schoen, D. E. (2020) *The war of the gods in addiction: C. G. Jung, Alcoholics Anonymous, and archetypal evil.* Chiron.

> In this book, there are five chapters. The first chapter contains the letters between Bill W. (one of the AA cofounders) and Carl Jung. The next two chapters review Jungian psychology concepts and how they relate to addiction. The fourth chapter intertwines the 12 steps of AA and Jungian psychology concepts. The final chapter is on the dreams of individuals with SUD and how they can be used by helping professionals working with clients with SUD.

Sharp, D. (1991). *Jung Lexicon: A primer of terms and concepts.* Inner City Books.

> This book focuses on understanding basic Jungian concepts, terms, and principles drawn from his *Collected Works* to demonstrate the broad scope/interpretation of Jungian psychology.

RESOURCES/WEBSITES

Gambling
Gamblers Anonymous (GA)

> https://gamblersanonymous.org/ga/

> This website contains psychoeducational information for individuals struggling with gambling and for counselors. These resources include locating meetings (e.g., in person, phone, virtual) in the United States and internationally; books/flyers/pamphlets, and so on; information on GA (e.g., description, history); a screening tool; and a monthly newsletter. It is based on the 12-step model of recovery.

Jungian Psychology (Direct Links)
Jungian Online

> https://www.jungianonline.com

> This website provides connections to Jungian analysts and psychotherapists throughout the world and information on Jungian psychology courses.

The Jung Page

> https://jungpage.org

> This website contains educational resources that include articles, books, audio, continuing education, and more. It facilitates connections with others interested in Jungian psychology (e.g., a blog).

The Society of Analytical Psychology (SAP)

> https://www.thesap.org.uk/articles-on-jungian-psychology-2/about-analysis-and-therapy/analytical-psychology/

> The SAP is the leading professional body for Jungian analysts and psychotherapists in the United Kingdom. Resources, such as journals, articles, trainings, and courses, are available.

Jungian Psychology (Connecting Links)
Links to Jungian sites

> http://www.jungnewyork.com/links.shtml

> This website has links to different Jungian association websites with a brief description of the website. There are also links describing the process of entering Jungian analysis and becoming a Jungian analyst as well as links to Jungian articles.

The C. G. Jung Center

> https://www.cgjungcenter.org/jungians-organizations/

> This link connects to a site that provides multiple links to different Jungian organizations in the United States and internationally. It contains online sources for study and discussion.

Credits

Fig. 4.1: Geri Miller, "Self-Care," *Academic Violence and Bullying of Faculty.* Copyright © 2023 by Cognella, Inc. Reprinted with permission.

Table 4.2a: Alcoholics Anonymous, Selection "How It Works," *Alcoholics Anonymous: The Story of How Many Thousands of Men and Women Have Recovered from Alcoholism*, pp. 71-72, Alcoholics Anonymous World Services, Inc., 1939.

Table 4.2: David E. Schoen, Selection from "The Healing Process of Recovery through the Twelve Steps of A.A.," *The War Of The Gods In Addiction: C. G. Jung, Alcoholics Anonymous, and Archetypal Evil*, p. 98. Copyright © 2020 by Chiron Publications.

Conclusion

I n conclusion, I hope this book has opened up new perspectives on looking at SUD and that dialogues, debates, and discussions among helping professionals have been encouraged. My hope is that compassion for people with SUD has been fueled by the views shared in this book and that the diagnosis and treatment of SUD is enhanced for the unique population served by the helping professional who reads this book.

I have, in essence, been gathering information and talking with others for over 40 years about SUD. Writing this book has changed me both personally and professionally. I hope that you, the reader, are also changed, like me, as a result of this book and are inspired to be

- gentler with self and others;
- humbled by the honor of working in the SUD field; and
- grateful for the gifts of *Eros*: light, goodness, and healing.

For as long as there is life in the person with SUD, then there is hope we can help them find their way into recovery.

I wish you the best in your important work with clients with SUD. Thank you for sharing the experience of this book with me. Perhaps our paths will cross again someday.

References

Ackerman, N. W. (1982). The art of family therapy. In D. Bolck & R. Simon (Eds.), *The strength of family therapy: Selected papers of Nathan W. Ackerman* (pp. 284–286). Brunner/Mazel. (Original work published 1970)

Alcoholics Anonymous. (1953). *Twelve steps and twelve traditions*. Alcoholics Anonymous World Services.

Alcoholics Anonymous. (1976). *Alcoholics Anonymous (3rd ed.)*. Alcoholics Anonymous World Services.

Alcoholics Anonymous. (1991). *Twelve steps and twelve traditions*. Alcoholics Anonymous World Services.

Alcoholics Anonymous. (2001). *Alcoholics Anonymous (4th ed.)*. Alcoholics Anonymous World Services

Allport, G. W. (1950). *The individual and his religion*. MacMillan.

American Music Therapy Association. (2021). *Music therapy and addiction treatment*. https://www.musictherapy.org/assets/1/7/FactSheet_Music_Therapy_and_Addiction_Treatment_2021.pdf

American Psychological Association. *Ethical Principles of Psychologists and Code of Conduct*. Washington, DC: American Psychological Association, 2017. https://www.apa.org/ethics/code/

American Psychiatric Association. (2013). *Diagnostic and statistical manual of mental disorders* (5th ed.).

Barton, J. (2019). *Addiction as archetype: Storytelling in drug addiction and recovery. Bad glue for broken bones: An addiction memoir* (Publication No. 28705626) [Master's thesis, Liverpool John Moores University]. ProQuest Dissertations & Theses Global. https://www.proquest.com/openview/29c3fd5651a7726a0fb001ea83eb7175/1?pq-origsite=gscholar&cbl=2026366&diss=y

Bell, H., Limberg, D., Jacobson, L., & Super, J. T. (2014) Enhancing self-awareness through creative experiential-learning play-based activities. *Journal of Creativity in Mental Health*, 9(3), 399–414. https://doi.org/10.1080/15401383.2014.897926

Berger, A. (2010). *12 smart things to do when the booze and drugs are gone*. Hazelden.

Berne, E. (1964). *The games people play: The psychology of human relationships*. Dell.

Betty Ford Institute Consensus Panel. (2007). What is recovery? A working definition from the Betty Ford Institute. *Journal of Substance Abuse Treatment, 33*(3), 221–228. https://doi.org/10.1016/j.jsat.2007.06.001

Big Think. (2014, December 5). *Leopold Stokowski: "Musicians paint their pictures on silence."* https://bigthink.com/words-of-wisdom/leopold-stokowski-musicians-paint-their-pictures-on-silence/#.~:text=Word%20of%20wisdom%20from%20the,paint%20their%20pictures%20on%20on%20silence.%22&text=Leopold%20Stokowski%20(1882%2D1977),the%20score%20for%20Disney%27s%20Fantasia

Bourdaghs, S., & Silverman, M. J. (2020). A neurological rationale for music therapy to address social connectivity among individuals with substance use disorders. *The Arts in Psychotherapy, 70*, Article 101681 https://doi.org/10.1016/j.aip.2020.101681

Broderick, P.C., & Blewitt, P. (2020). *The life span: Human development for helping professionals* (5th ed.). Pearson.

Buerger, W. M., & Miller, A. L. (2022). Humor, irreverent communication, and DBT. In R. D. Friedberg & E. V. Rozmid (Eds.), *Creative CBT with youth*(25-41. Cham: Springer International Publishing. https://doi.org/10.1007/978-3-030-99669-7_3

Canha, R. (2016, April). Using humor in treatment of substance use disorders: Worthy of further investigation. *The Open Nursing Journal, 10*, 37–44. https://doi.org/10.2174/1874434601610010037

Canha, R. (2020). Humor and opioid recovery (Publication No. 13896490) [Doctoral dissertation, University of Maryland–Baltimore]. ProQuest.

Canning, P. (2021). *Killing season: A paramedic's dispatches from the front lines of the opioid epidemic.* John Hopkins University Press.

Carter, T. E., & Panisch, L. S. (2021). A systematic review of music therapy for psychosocial outcomes of substance use clients. *International Journal of Mental Health and Addiction, 19*, 1551–1568. https://doi.org/10.1007/s11469-020-00246-8

Clark, A. A. (2014). Narrative therapy integration within substance abuse groups, *Journal of Creativity in Mental Health, 9*(4), 511–522.

Compton, L., & Patterson, T. (2023, September). Essential skill development for meaningful social connection. *Counseling Today, 66,* 41–45.

Corey, G. (2017). *Theory and practice of counseling and psychology* (10th ed.). Cengage.

Craigen, L. M. (2023, July). Integrating psychological flow in counseling. *Counseling Today, 66,* 45–48.

Csikszentmihalyi, M. (1999). If we are so rich, why aren't we happy? *American Psychologist, 54*(10), 821–827. https://doi.org/10.1037/0003-066X.54.10.821

Davidson, L. J. (2019). *From darkness to light: An exploration of self-discovery and healing through collaborative recovery expressive* writing (Publication No. 2311919043) [Doctoral dissertation, Marshall University]. ProQuest Central; ProQuest Dissertations & Theses Global; ProQuest One Literature..

Dayton, T. (2007). *Emotional sobriety.* Health Communications.

Dingle, G. A., Gleadhill, L., & Baker, F. A. (2008). Can music therapy engage patients in group cognitive behaviour therapy for substance abuse treatment? *Drug and Alcohol Review, 27,* 190–196. https://doi.org/10.1080/09595230701829371

Dixon, N. F. (1980). Humor: A cognitive alternative to stress? In I. G. Sarason, & C. D. Spielberger (Eds.), *Stress and anxiety* (Vol. 7, pp. 281–289). Hemisphere.

Fancourt, D., & Finn, S. (2019). *What is the evidence on the role of the arts in improving health and wellbeing? A scoping review. World Health Organization.* https://iris.who.int/handle/10665/329834.

Freud, S. (1959). Humor. In J. Strachey (Ed.), *Collected papers of Sigmund Freud* (Vol. 5). Basic Books.

Freud, S. (1960). *Jokes and their relation to the unconscious.* Norton.

Galvani, S., G., Roy, A., & Clayson, A. (Ed.) (2022). *Long-term recovery from substance use: European perspectives.* Policy Press.

Gamblers Anonymous. (2007). *Gamblers Anonymous.*

Gardstrom, S. C. (2021). *Music as a trigger for substance abuse.* In S. C. Gardstrom & J. Willenbrink-Conte, (Eds.), *Music therapy with women with addictions.* Barcelona Publishers.

Gardstrom, S. C., & Diestelkamp, W. S. (2013). Women with addictions report reduced anxiety after group music therapy: A quasi-experimental study. *Voices: A World Forum for Music Therapy, 13*(2). https://doi.org/10.15845/voices.v13i2.681

Gardstrom, S. C., Klemm, A., & Murphy, K. M. (2017). Women's perceptions of the usefulness of group music therapy in addictions recovery. *Nordic Journal of Music Therapy, 26*(4), 338–358. https://doi.org/10.1080/08098131.2016.1239649

Goldin, E., Bordan, T., Araoz, D. L., Gladding, S. T., Kaplan, D., Krumboltz, J., & Lazarus, A. (2006). Humor in counseling: Leader perspectives. *Journal of Counseling & Development, 84*(4), 397–404.

Gramlich, J. (2022, January 19). *Recent surge in U.S. drug overdose deaths has hit Black men the hardest.* Pew Research Center. https://www.pewresearch.org/short-reads/2022/01/19/recent-surge-in-u-s-drug-overdose-deaths-has-hit-black-men-the-hardest/

Gul, M., & Aqeel, M. (2021). Acceptance and commitment therapy for treatment of stigma and shame in substance use disorders: A double-blind, parallel-group, randomized controlled trial, *Journal of Substance Use, 26*(4), 413–419. https://doi.org/10.1080/14659891.2020.1846803

Hall, C. S., & Nordby, V. J. (1999). *A primer of Jungian psychology.* Meridian.

Hart, C. H., & Ksir, C. J. (2018). *Drugs, society, & human behavior* (18th ed.). McGraw Hill.

Hawk, K. M. (2022). *Creativity towards Resilience: Liberation, community, and the open studio with substance using transitional aged youth* (Publication No. 26469078II) [Master's thesis, Pacifica Graduate Institute]. ProQuest Dissertations & Theses Global. https://www.proquest.com/open-view/3a1f8e3b999b516471de14c76a95ba38/1.pdf?pq-origsite=gscholar&cbl=18750&diss=y

Heiden, L. E. (2008). *Play therapy with adults* (Publication No. 833) [Master's thesis, University of Northern Iowa]. ScholarWorks. https://scholarworks.uni.edu/grp/833

Hiller, J., & Gardstrom, S. (2019, March 19). Warning: Music therapy comes with risks. *OUPblog.* https://blog.oup.com/2019/03/warning-music-therapy-risks/

Hohmann, J., Stegemann, T., & Koelsch, S. (2017). Effects of music therapy and music-based interventions in the treatment of substance use disorders: A systematic review. *PloS One, 12*(11), e0187363–e0187363. https://doi.org/10.1371/journal.pone.0187363

Jenkins, K. (1998). *The world of river otters.* Pathways to Nature Publications.

Judd, H., Meier, C. L., Yaugher, A. C., & Atismé-Vebins, K. (2023). Opioid use disorder stigma reduction through story telling narrative and sharing: A qualitative review and lessons learned. *International Journal of Mental Health and Addiction, 21*(1), 468–483. https://doi.org/10.1007/s11469-021-00606-y

Kelly, J. F. (2004). Toward an addictionary: A proposal for more precise terminology. *Alcoholism Treatment Quarterly, 22,* 79–87.

Kelly, J. F., Saitz, R., & Wakeman, S. (2016). Language, substance use disorders, and policy. The need to reach consensus on an "addiction-ary." *Alcoholism Treatment Quarterly, 34,* 116–123.

Leung, H., Shek, D. T. L., Yu, L., Wu, F. K. Y., Law, M. Y. M., Chan, E. M. L., & Lo, C. K. M. (2018). Evaluation of "Colorful Life": A multi-addiction expressive arts intervention program for adolescents of addicted parents and parents with addiction. *International Journal of Mental Health and Addiction, 16*(6), 1343–1356. https://doi.org/10.1007/s11469-018-9899-3

Malvini Redden, S., Tracy, S. J., & Shafer, M. S. (2013). A metaphor analysis of recovering substance abusers' sensemaking of medication-assisted treatment. *Qualitative Health Research, 23*(7), 951–962.

Martin, R. A. (2007). *The psychology of humor: An integrative approach.* Elsevier.

Martin, R., & Kuiper, N. (2016). Three decades investigating humor and laughter: An interview with professor Martin. *Europe's Journal of Psychology*, *12(3)*, 498–512.

Martin, R., & Lefcourt, H. (1983). Sense of humor as a moderator of the relation between stressors and mood. *Journal of Personality and Social Psychology*, *45(6)*, 1313–1324.

Martinelli, T. F., Nagelhout, G. E., Bellaert, L., Best, D., Vanderplasschen, W., & van de Mheen, D. (2020). Comparing three stages of addiction recovery: Long-term recovery and its relation to housing problems, crime, occupation situation, and substance use. *Drugs: Education, Prevention and Policy*, *27(5)*, 387–396. 10.1080/09687637.2020.1779182

Maslow, A. H. (1998). *Maslow on management*. Wiley.

May, R. (1953). *Man's search for himself*. Norton.

McNally, M., & Cochrane, B. (October, 2023). *Ethical & Legal Decision-Making for Psychologists*. North Carolina Psychological Association Workshop.

Miller, G. (2021). *Learning the language of addiction counseling* (5th ed.). Wiley.

Miller, G. (2023, May 3–5). *Group counseling and group community building: Motivational interviewing focus* [Paper presentation]. Women's Recovery Conference, Asheville, NC, United States.

Miller, G. (2024). *Academic violence and bullying of faculty*. Cognella Academic Publishing.

Miller, W. R., Forcehimes, A. A., & Zweben, A. (2019). *Treating addiction: A guide for professionals* (2nd ed.). Guilford.

Miller, W. R., & Rollnick, S. (2013). *Motivational interviewing* (3rd ed.). Guilford.

Moghadam, M. P., Balouchi, S. M., Madarshahian, F., & Moghadam, K. (2016). Effects of storytelling-based education in the prevention of drug abuse among adolescents in Iran based on a readiness to addiction index. *Journal of Clinical and Diagnostic Research, 10*(11), IC06–IC09. https://doi.org/10.7860/JCDR/2016/23170.8799

Moyers, W. C. (2006). *Broken: My Story of Addiction and Redemption*. Viking.

National Institute on Drug Abuse. (2022, August 22). *Marijuana and hallucinogen use among young adults reached an all-time high in 2021*. https://nida.nih.gov/news-events/news-releases/2022/08/marijuana-and-hallucinogen-use-among-young-adults-reached-all-time-high-in-2021

Nordfjaern, T. (2011). Relapse patterns among patients with substance use disorders. *Journal of Substance Use, 16*(4), 313–329. https://doi.org/10.3109/14659890903580482

Odabaş, M. (2022, May 31). *Concern about drug addiction has declined in U.S., even in areas where fatal overdoses have risen the most*. Pew Research Center. https://www.pewresearch.org/short-reads/2022/05/31/concern-about-

drug-addiction-has-declined-in-u-s-even-in-areas-where-fatal-overdoses-
have-risen-the-most/#:~:text=The%20share%20of%20Americans%20who,
rates%20have%20increased%20the%20most.

Park, J. W., & Kim, H. S. (2023). The effects of group counseling utilizing narrative therapy on self-esteem, stress response, and insight for individuals with alcohol dependency. *Journal of Creativity in Mental Health*, *18*(2), 219–248.

Paterno, M. T., Fiddian-Green, A., & Gubrium, A. (2018). Moms supporting moms: Digital storytelling with peer mentors in recovery from substance use. *Health Promotion Practice*, 19(6), 823–832.

Quercus (Ed.). (2006). *The greatest American speeches*. Quercus.

Rhodes, L. R. (2024, January). Happy days. *Counseling Today*, 36–42.

Ricks, L., Kitchens, S., Goodrich, T., & Hancock, E. (2014). My story: The use of narrative therapy in individual and group counseling. *Journal of Creativity in Mental Health*, *9*(1), 99–110.

Ross, D., & Collins, P. (2010). Defining addiction and identifying the public interest in liberal democracies. In D. Ross, H. Kincaid, D. Spurrett, & P. Collins (Eds.), *What is addiction?* MIT Press.

Roy, A., Galvani, S., & Clayson, A. (2022). Recovery as long term: An introduction. In S. Galvani, A. Roy, & A. Clayson (Eds.), *Long-term recovery from substance use: European perspectives* (pp. 3–14). Policy Press.

Russell, A. M., Bergman, B. G., Colditz, J. B., Kelly, J. F., Milaham, P. J., & Massey, P. M. (2021). *Using TikTok in recovery from substance use disorder. Drug and Alcohol Dependence,* 229(Part A), Article 109147. https://doi.org/10.1016/j.drugalcdep.2021.109147.

Schenker, M. D. (2009). *A clinician's guide to 12-step recovery: Integrating 12-step programs into psychotherapy.* Norton.

Schoen, D. E. (2020) *The war of the gods in addiction: C. G. Jung, Alcoholics Anonymous, and archetypal evil.* Chiron.

Schumacher, J. A., & Williams, D. C. (2020). *Psychological treatment of medical patients struggling with harmful substance use.* American Psychological Association.

Sharp, D. (1991). *Jung Lexicon: A primer of terms and concepts: A primer of terms & concepts.* Inner City Books.

Silverman, M. J. (2022). *Music therapy in mental health for illness management and recovery* (2nd ed.). Oxford University Press.

Situmorang, D. D. B. (2020). Music therapy for the treatment of patients with addictions in COVID-19 pandemic. *Addictive Disorders & Their Treatment*, *19*(4), 252. https://doi.org/10.1097/ADT.0000000000000224

Soshensky, R. (2001). Music therapy and addiction, *Music Therapy Perspectives*, *19*(1), 45–52. https://doi.org/10.1093/mtp/19.1.45

Stromberg, G., & Merrill, C. (2005). *The harder they fall*. Hazelden.

Stuebing, M. D., Lorenz, H., & Littlefield, L. M. (2020). Literacy-Free 12 Step Expressive Arts Curriculum enhances engagement and treatment outcomes for dually diagnosed literature review substance use and mental health disorders. *Alcoholism Treatment Quarterly, 38*(2), 250–265. https://doi.org/1 0.1080/07347324.2019.1681331

Substance Abuse and Mental Health Services. (n.d.). *2022 National Survey on Drug Use and Health (NSDUH) releases.* Retrieved June 22, 2023, from https://www.samhsa.gov/data/sites/default/files/reports/rpt42731/2022-nsduh-main-highlights.pdf

Substance Abuse and Mental Health Services Administration. (2021). *Key substance use and mental health indicators in the United States: Results from the 2020 National Survey on Drug Use and Health* (HHS Publication No. PEP21-07-01-003, NSDUH Series H-56). Center for Behavioral Health Statistics and Quality. https://www.samhsa.gov/data/sites/default/files/reports/rpt35325/NSDUHFFRPDFWHTMLFiles2020/2020NSDUHF-FR1PDFW102121.pdf

Sultanoff, S. M. (2013). Integrating humor into psychotherapy: Research, theory, and the necessary conditions for the presence of therapeutic humor in helping relationships. *The Humanistic Psychologist, 41,* 388–399.

Tam, H., Shik, A. W., & Lam, S. S. (2016). Using expressive arts in relapse prevention of young psychotropic substance abusers in Hong Kong. *Children and Youth Services Review, 60,* 88–100. https://doi.org/10.1016/j.childyouth.2015.11.022

Taylor, M. (2023, August). A mental wellness program for law enforcement. *Counseling Today, 66,* 34–38.

Thompson, S., Deaner, K., & Franco, M. G. (2023). How to help clients make friends. *Journal of Health Service Psychology, 49,* 75–83.

Tiebout, H. (1999). *Harry Tiebout: The collected writings.* Hazelden.

United Nations Office on Drugs and Crime. (2022). *World Drug Report 2022.* https://www.unodc.org/unodc/en/data-and-analysis/world-drug-report-2022.html

Vanderplasschen, W., & Best, D. (2021). Mechanisms and mediators of addiction recovery. *Drugs: Education, Prevention and Policy, 28*(5), 385–388. https://doi.org/10.1080/09687637.2021.1982521

Walsh, D., & Koch, G. (2023, November). Helping clients navigate religious trauma. *Counseling Today,* 33–37.

Walsh, T. (2008). *Wham-O Super Book.* Chronicle Books

Warren, J. A., Hof, K. R., McGriff, D., & Morris, L. B. (2012) Five experiential learning activities in addictions education. *Journal of Creativity in Mental Health, 7*(3), 272–288. https://doi.org/10.1080/15401383.2012.710172

Weir, (2017, October). The power of restorative sleep. *Monitor on Psychology, 48*(9), 39–43.

Williams, T. (2023). Substance abuse treatment, critical race theory, and counter-storytelling for the Black emerging adult male. *Journal of Racial and Ethnic Health Disparities, 11,* 1067–1076. https://doi.org/10.1007/s40615-023-01586-6

Wilson, B. (1958, January). The next frontier: Emotional sobriety. *AA Grapevine.*

Wulbert, P. R. (2018). The use of storytelling in recovery for college students with substance use disorders [Doctoral dissertation, The University of Texas at Austin]. Texas ScholarWorks.

Yalom, I. (1985). *The theory and practice of group psychotherapy* (3rd ed.). Basic Books.

Index

www.ingramcontent.com/pod-product-compliance
Lightning Source LLC
Chambersburg PA
CBHW050654280326
41932CB00015B/2900